The Right Mix

The Right Mix

How to Pick Mutual Funds for Your Portfolio

Howard Keller

Harvey Sontag

McGraw-Hill, Inc.

New York St. Louis San Francisco Auckland Bogotá
Caracas Lisbon London Madrid Mexico Milan
Montreal New Delhi Paris San Juan São Paulo
Singapore Sydney Tokyo Toronto

Library of Congress Cataloging-in-Publication Data

Keller, Howard.
　　The right mix: how to pick mutual funds for your portfolio
　/　Howard Keller, Harvey Sontag.
　　　　p.　　cm.
　　Includes index.
　　ISBN 0-07-033746-2　　　—ISBN 0-07-033785-3 (pbk.)
　　1. Mutual funds.　2. Investments.
　　3. Portfolio management.　I. Sontag, Harvey.　II. Title.
　　HG4530.K45　1993
　　332.63′27—dc20　　　　　　　　　　　　　　　92-23566
　　　　　　　　　　　　　　　　　　　　　　　　　　　　CIP

1 2 3 4 5 6 7 8 9 0　DOC/DOC　9 8 7 6 5 4 3 2

ISBN 0-07-033746-2 {HC}
ISBN 0-07-033785-3 {PBK}

*The sponsoring editor for this book was David Conti, the editing supervisor was
Caroline Levine, and the production supervisor was Donald F. Schmidt. This
book was set in Baskerville by Carol Woolverton, Lexington, Mass., in
cooperation with Warren Publishing Services.*

Printed and bound by R. R. Donnelley & Sons Company.

Contents

Preface

Most potential investors in mutual funds find more information available than they can easily use or understand. This book will help you blast through all other information about mutual funds, figure out where you want to go, and create a customized portfolio to meet your needs.

Here you will learn how to evaluate your current financial needs, assess your current situation, plan for the future, and pick the right mix of mutual funds for your portfolio. Here we provide a programmatic approach which leads you through a self-assessment using questionnaires and worksheets. Then, when you have established specific financial goals, you proceed to construct an investment plan. Based on your investment plan, you carry out a systematic and comprehensive selection of no-load mutual funds which will create a portfolio to meet your personal investment objectives.

This book is intended for those who want to invest but need some practical guidance to get started or who have tried to invest but have been dissatisfied with the results. Here is a straightforward, concise guide to starting a practical investment program centered on no-load and low-load mutual funds. Included are basic concepts such as the many types of funds and how to invest in them, what types of returns to expect, how to determine your individualized investment goals, other factors to consider before investing, how to choose specific funds, how to allocate your investments among your chosen funds, how to handle the mechanics of investing in these funds, how to evaluate your results, and what to do next.

Mutual funds are an advantageous way for the individual to invest in securities, offering diversification, liquidity, and professional management. A portfolio of mutual funds can be tailored to suit individual goals and needs. Purchasing no-load and low-load funds is a cost-effective way to invest in mutual funds.

The book is designed for all those people who have some money to invest but face a dilemma: Since they are not trained in investing they feel lost when it comes time to invest their hard-earned money. They are dependent on others to advise them but do not know how to find someone in whom they can have confidence. Most of them do not have the hundreds of thousands of dollars that would be required to hire a top financial advisor. Many do not want to trust their futures and divulge their personal matters to someone whom they do not know well. They have heard about financial planners and advisors who failed to do a good job for their clients—or worse, who lost (even stole) clients' funds. Furthermore, they do not want to spend substantial sums of money for advice that might prove to be superficial or inadequate. These investors are looking for a realistic way to get clear, concise advice on how to plan their finances in order to develop an investment program.

One-quarter of a billion Americans represent a vast spectrum of financial situations and needs. Any attempt to shoehorn these widely differing people into a few groups and treat the members of a group alike is doomed to failure. Experience has shown that many investment plans fail to deal with all the relevant facts in an attempt to force people into their cookie cutter plans or simplified computer programs. The authors recognize the need for flexibility in dealing with the vast range of people and their situations and offer a step-by-step approach that will help readers evaluate their own needs, set investment goals, and create successful investment plans closely tailored to their unique situations.

The method presented here is not the only way to invest, but it is an effective approach that can be used by the nonprofessional to create a workable plan without a great investment of time or money. Furthermore, the plan can be adapted to a broad range of changing needs and circumstances, and it can become the first stepping stone to more elaborate investment plans for those who want to go beyond the scope of this book.

Howard Keller
Harvey Sontag

Acknowledgments

The authors would like to express thanks for the help of the following people in preparing the manuscript. We appreciate their time and effort in reviewing, critiquing, and suggesting improvements, as well as other support and assistance they provided.

Eraina Cocomero

Karen Crandall

Eileen DeFreest

Sheldon Jacobs

Keith Keller

LaRue Keller

Helen Louie

Rosemary Rush

Joyce Hamm Sontag

We especially appreciate the efforts of David Conti and Carol Levine of McGraw-Hill toward the publication of this book.

The Right Mix

Introduction

Like Gaul, this book is divided into parts. In Part 1, "Self-Assessment," you will evaluate your financial needs, preferences, goals, and priorities and develop an investment strategy. In Part 2, "Mutual Fund Basics," you will develop an understanding of how mutual funds operate and learn the basic background information you will need as an investor. In Part 3, "Portfolio Selection," you will learn how to implement the investment strategy you developed in Part 1 by choosing a portfolio of mutual funds using a systematic approach. In Part 4, "Additional Resources and Other Topics," you will find a comprehensive discussion of fund families and a guide to print, computer, and other resources.

Basics

This book makes some basic assumptions about its readers and about investing that we would like to spell out here.

1. You will not be able to reliably predict the future. Experience supports this assertion. Futurists and highly paid Wall Street gurus have demonstrated repeatedly that they are generally unable to do so despite their hard work or their claims of success. Although each Wall Street debacle or bull market is followed by people who claim to have predicted it, the next major move often shows these "experts" to be wrong. Apparently, their original successes owe more to luck than to knowledge.

2. Tomorrow will not be exactly like yesterday, so that although the track records of funds will be a help in finding good funds to invest in, they will not be a sure guide to future performance. The book shows how and why some funds do well for a while, then become poor performers. It leads the reader through techniques for identifying candidates for good performance.

3. The stock market is largely unpredictable and is affected in the short term by many noneconomic events such as the illness or death of a political leader, a major development in foreign affairs, panic reactions, and computerized-trading induced volatility. But over a long enough period, many studies have shown that the returns on stocks are very likely to be much higher than the returns from all other types of investments. Furthermore, studies have shown that the volatile downward moves of the market have usually been offset by market rises to at least the former levels within two years. So, although you cannot be sure what the market will do tomorrow or next week, you can put the odds in your favor for the long haul. As Damon Runyon once said, "The battle is not always to the strong, or the race to the swift—but that's the way to bet."

The design of the book is flexible enough to cover a broad range of investment needs and to adjust to your needs as your level of knowledge and interest grows. If you reach a stage where you want to try investments other than mutual funds, the book will help suggest some additional investment ideas and sources of knowledge about them.

A goal-oriented investment approach is employed here. It assumes that the initial step in making any investment plan is to establish a goal. Goals can be general or specific. The goal could be to earn a high return over a specified time or to have an initial sum ($1000 for example) grow to some amount ($5000 for example) in a definite time. *But determining the nature of the goal and the period for its achievement are the initial crucial steps to creating a plan.*

Some typical goals might include: (1) saving for retirement (in 10 years, 20 years, etc.); (2) saving to buy a house ($20,000 needed in 10 years); (3) faster growth of my investments than is possible with bank CDs—say, one-half of my $20,000 of savings to stay in the bank, one-half to be put in an investment plan based on this book (the money is long-term investment money that is not going to be needed to pay bills over the next 10 years or so); (4) money to supplement retirement income needed in 2 years or so; (5) investing a specified sum for as much growth as possible over the next 20 years for college, or a wedding, or to start a business, or just for a nest egg.

Another key aspect of the book's approach is to help you evaluate your capacity to accept risk in relationship to other key investment characteristics. In general, high-return investments carry relatively high risk. But how much risk should you take to get a higher rate of return? The book presents a questionnaire and shows how to use the results of that questionnaire as input to your investment plan. The amount of risk you want to take is a crucial factor in determining how to invest and will influence the percentage of total assets that you will allocate to various investments at the different risk levels.

Why Mutual Funds?

Mutual funds fill an important need for the small investor. They provide a way to pool relatively small amounts of money with money from many other investors. The pooled money is managed by professional investment advisors. Each share owner participates in the gains (or losses) of the fund to the extent of his or her ownership (number of shares). The share values can be readily determined and their performance tracked, since they are published daily in the financial pages of newspapers. The funds are invested in a diversified portfolio of securities. The extent of diversification and the type of securities held by the fund depend on the objectives of the fund.

The funds are highly liquid. As with stocks, a phone call is sufficient to start the process of selling all or part of your investment and getting cash. Unlike stocks, the funds are "redeemed" by fund managers rather than sold to another investor. The price of the shares is determined each day by adding the value of all the securities and other investment assets held by the fund at the end of the day and dividing by the number of shares. This calculation gives the per-share value (or net asset value) which you can read in the paper the following day.

The Advantage of No-Load and Low-Load Funds

No-load funds, the ones of primary interest to readers of this book, are bought and sold at the net asset value. In other words, there is no charge to buy the funds, so you can buy the shares (from the firm that manages them) at the same price for which you would sell them back to the management firm.

In contrast, load funds have one price to buy and a different (lower) price to sell back. This means, for example, if you bought a fund with an 8 percent load and immediately sold it back to the fund manager, you would get 92 cents of each dollar back.

A $1000 purchase of an 8 percent load fund would be bought back for $920 on the same day. The disadvantage of load funds is immediately obvious. Your fund must increase in value just to get you even with your initial investment. Of course, if your load fund has an exceptional management, it may well be worthwhile to pay the load to "buy" the superior management. Over time a slightly better return will compound to a large difference, which could more than make up for the initial penalty of paying the load. This is something all investors have to consider if they find an attractive load fund that they want to invest in. Such factors as the length of time you expect to hold the fund and your estimate of the difference in return will be important.

For the most part, this book does not consider load funds. According to *Money* magazine as of the summer of 1990 there were about 3500 mutual funds. These include not just equity funds but also money market funds, funds that invest in bonds, funds that allocate the investment money (among stocks, bonds, and cash) and other special types of funds. With such a wealth of funds, many of which are no-load, this book chooses to concentrate on no-load funds. Studies have shown that load funds and no-load funds have performed equally well over time, with outstanding performers occurring in both groups.

PART 1
Self-Assessment

In Part 1 you will get a chance to evaluate your needs and preferences for investment risk, growth, income, and tax avoidance.
You will learn about your financial priorities, discover insights about your own circumstances and resources, and set the stage for developing a profitable investment program. The information you discover about yourself will enable you to develop an investment strategy to achieve your financial goals and to write a long-term investment plan.

1

Taking a Look at Your Personal Investment Preferences and Needs

In this chapter you will consider your financial preferences and needs and how time affects these factors. You will examine the steps you should take before beginning an investment program by using up-to-date self-evaluation techniques.

What Are the Key Factors of an Investment Program?

An investment program must be tailored to the objectives it will serve. In general, six major features describe investment plans: risk avoidance, growth potential, income potential, liquidity, diversification, and tax avoidance. The overriding goal is to create and manage an investment portfolio that provides you with an appropriate balance of these characteristics. Whether the balance achieved is appropriate depends on both your needs and the characteristics of the investment program that has been devised to meet those needs. Obviously, everyone's ideal would be to invest at no risk with the highest possible levels attainable of all other features, but such a goal would be unrealistic. In this chapter we will consider the meaning of each of these important features of investments in order to build a foundation for under-

7

standing how you can assess your investment needs and preferences. These needs and preferences will be the basis of selection for a mutual fund investment program described in subsequent chapters.

On a practical level, the market for investments, especially securities, offers investors the opportunity to purchase, at a specified price, an interrelated mix of features associated with a given investment at a particular time. The mix of features for each potential investment changes over time in response to changing conditions affecting the markets. For this reason, each investor needs to choose the particular set of trade-offs that are best for his or her own needs and circumstances at the time of evaluation within the constraints of the marketplace.

Part of the problem of creating a well-chosen portfolio may be in deciding what market or markets to trade in. Not every investment has to be in securities, and you may want to consider other areas. For example, you might want to consider the alternatives of actively investing in real estate, buying a partnership in a small business (such as a restaurant or dry cleaning shop), or buying stamps or antiques. If you are knowledgeable about a particular real estate market in a nearby community or a type of business or professional field, an investment of this kind gives you personal responsibility for the success or failure of the enterprise. Such investments can have both economic and emotional rewards, such as satisfaction for a job well done or for providing a valuable service or product to the community; such investments can also have many risks and problems.

When you purchase individual securities, such as stocks or bonds, the options for controlling the fate of your investments are more limited because only the decisions of what to buy and when to buy or sell are exclusively your own. When you purchase securities through mutual fund ownership, you are yet another level removed from day-to-day management of investment activities, and your decisions have to be taken broadly. The investor at this level faces problems in acquiring expertise about whole classes of investments in diverse markets, communities, and nations. Fortunately, an army of professional analysts and reporters works diligently to gather and convey expertise through an assortment of channels in the press and other media and through brokerage house research departments.

It is the job of the mutual fund manager to take advantage of the available information and use it to make specific buying decisions. For you to make wise choices among the many available mutual funds, you must have some general understanding about investment characteristics and their interrelationships.

Risk Avoidance

There are as many types of risk as there are possibilities for losing money. For investors in securities and other resalable investments, the market risk consists of the likelihood that the market value of holdings will diminish. Reductions in market value are determined by many factors. One important factor may be a change in investors' attitudes toward the worth of an entire class of assets. This phenomenon is known as a "bear market" and usually reflects other underlying beliefs about the state of the economy; however, an important component is simply the psychology of investors—widespread perceptions that "the market is headed down."

These perceptions may or may not be based on real economic changes, such as changing interest rates. An example in terms of bonds might be a general reduction in bond prices associated with an increase in interest rates, reflecting the relatively lower earning power of existing debt securities in comparison to the new, higher interest rates. A similar example in terms of common stock could occur in anticipation of the dampening effects higher interest rates have on the economy. In real estate, since financing costs represent a major segment of the expenses of owning and operating property, a change in interest rates will directly affect market value. With an increasing burden of debt evident in many corporations across many industries, the costs of financing and refinancing also are increased as interest charges rise. This has a direct effect on corporate earnings, and indirectly an effect on market values of corporate bonds and common stock.

In one sense, these examples illustrate how a change in the particular economic variable of interest rates can cut across several categories of assets. But market perceptions can also be fueled by fears (of war, of social or political problems) or by hopes (opportunities resulting from the collapse of communism, anticipation of peaceful times and good economic conditions) and other less tangible forces than economics.

More specifically, an important form of risk can arise from having your investments concentrated in particular industries or geographical regions that may be economically depressed while the rest of the country does well. Alternatively, such regions might be struck by some major disaster such as an earthquake or hurricane.

This risk which arises from failure to spread your investments is called *failure to diversify*. The possibility of problems in the oil industry at the beginning of the 1980s was primarily a risk for a limited region of the United States, the Southwest. But when the potential of those risks began to be realized and actual economic losses multiplied throughout the economy of that region, the risks began affecting not only the oil business but real estate, thrifts, and virtually all segments of the economy of the region. Although, through the intervention of federal deposit insurance, the cost of paying for these losses in this particular case will ultimately be spread throughout the entire country's economy, an individual investor's risk in investing in the oil industry was initially localized to a particular industry, region, and period.

When an investment is made in the securities of a specific company, additional risks are associated with both the historical and current management and financial position of that unique organization. The company may own worthless assets, have acquired excessive debts, lose business and income, face strikes or adverse changes in government regulation; the company may be well managed but overwhelmed by superior competition, new technologies, or unexpected developments beyond its control as in the case of the Tylenol scares at Johnson and Johnson.

Most mutual funds effectively reduce risks associated with specific companies, industries, and geographical regions by diversifying investments. The funds buy shares in companies in various industries and regions to avoid excessive concentration of risk. Still, they are affected by market-level risks, although an investment strategy may be devised to hedge against overall changes in market values. Some types of funds try to lessen the effect of market changes by varying their asset mix from time to time in reaction to market changes.

Apart from market risks, there are other risks to consider. These include risks resulting from inflation, which threatens the purchasing power of your invested money, risks from events in a particular country or global region, as well as the associated currency rate risk. Although in general you will seek to reduce risk as much as possible, in some situations you may not want to reduce risks through diversification because, by concentrating assets in specific industries or countries where you expect rapid growth, you enhance possibilities for high returns. Some types of funds called "sector funds" are based on this concept.

Growth

Sometimes you may want to take more risk to achieve faster growth. *Growth,* for purposes of this book, is defined as an increase in your invested capital, either as a result of market appreciation or because of accumulated interest and dividends over time. As with risk, a variety of similar considerations apply. One class of assets (bonds, stocks, real estate, etc.) may appreciate more rapidly than others during a particular period. Alternatively, general economic factors, such as interest rate changes, may have overall effects on many types of assets. Specific industries may rise and fall, both as a result of economic conditions and variations in supply and demand related to other influences such as population shifts, technological developments, or even favorable or unfavorable weather patterns. On the individual company level, quality of management is again a critical factor that can change unpredictably and that may be difficult to evaluate. *Using mutual funds as a vehicle for investment makes growth somewhat predictable by smoothing gains and profits across companies and/or industries.* This is due to the good (and bad) results of investments from many companies being added together, thus lessening the effect of any one company. But opportunities for windfalls and very rapid growth are also diminished.

Income

Most people think of *income* as spendable money. Of course, it is entirely possible to join a sum of money, investment projections of risk and growth, and predictions of longevity to produce a guaranteed stream of income while liquidating your principal, as in the case of an annuity. Some investments only partially convert capital to income, such as "Ginnie Mae" securities, which return both principal and interest to the investor. Investors generally cannot achieve high growth, low risk, and high income all in one investment or group of investments. Trade-offs are frequently required to optimize one characteristic while accepting a less than optimal value of some other trait. High income may sometimes be achieved at the expense of high risk and low growth, or low risk and high growth can be attained while income is low. Or relatively low income may be accepted to achieve some tax advantage. Your choice of trade-offs depends on the nature of your personal goals and needs as well as on the character of your investments. *Mutual funds can make these choices easier by making them more obvious.*

Liquidity

Liquidity is the ability to rapidly convert your investment back to cash whenever you wish to. Major securities, including listed stocks and bonds of corporations and the U.S. government and many stocks of larger companies traded over the counter, are liquid. You can call your broker any day that the stock markets are in session and dispose of your investment that same day. Some small company stocks that are traded over the counter are much less liquid. They trade infrequently, and getting a firm quotation of the price is difficult. Often transaction costs are very high as well.

Many stock brokerage firms currently offer an account which carries the idea of liquidity even further with a combination of services including a VISA or MasterCard card with credit limits secured by your invested assets. They offer check-writing privileges combined with money market fund investments. This type of investment arrangement is almost as liquid as cash in your wallet. *One great advantage of mutual funds is that you can quickly convert your funds to cash by redeeming shares or borrow against them with ease under most circumstances.* In contrast, an investment in real estate may fluctuate from highly illiquid, during depressed market years when bank lending practices reflect cynicism about appraised values, to relatively more liquid during periods of easy money and growth in real estate prices, when banks are more willing to lend and buyers more willing to purchase. But even in times of rapidly escalating property values, it may take several weeks to several months between the time you decide to sell and the time you hold the money in your hand.

Diversification

Many investors consider diversification to be the "sine qua non" of mutual fund investing. Although you could, in theory, achieve a sufficient level of diversification by investing in the stocks and bonds of many industries and companies, the capital required would be beyond the means of the average investor.

International mutual funds allow an unsophisticated investor to achieve cultural and geographical diversification, either by investing in funds of one country or geographical area or by investing in many countries. Currency fluctuations may introduce yet another source of risk and opportunity associated with these investments.

Another possibility to consider is diversification by purchasing mutual funds which hold different classes of assets within specialized portfolios. For example, depending on economic conditions, you might shift the proportions of your holdings among precious metals, fixed income, real estate, oil and gas, utility, and science and technology funds.

The sector fund concentrates on specific industries thereby restricting diversification and its protection against loss while increasing growth potential. Often a single sponsor will offer a variety of these funds, which allow an investor more choice in structuring a portfolio because they are less diversified than more general mutual funds.

Tax Avoidance

If your investment program is successful, you do not necessarily have to pay taxes on the growth or income derived from profitable investments. *Mutual funds can be very helpful in multiplying options for lawful tax avoidance for the unsophisticated investor.*

Tax-Free Money Market Funds

Because they invest in tax-exempt securities, such as debt issued by state and municipal government, the income derived from these funds is not subject to federal taxation and will not be taxed within the state of origin. Most of these funds are readily convertible to cash and offer check-writing privileges.

U.S. Government Bond Funds

Although interest paid on U.S. government treasury bonds and notes is subject to federal taxation, it is exempt from state and local taxes.

Tax-Exempt Municipal Bond Funds

These enjoy the same tax benefits as tax-free money market funds (exemption from federal, state, and local taxes) but tend to offer higher yields and greater risks because of their investment in long-term issues.

In addition, when purchasing any other type of mutual fund, *judicious timing may avoid unexpected tax liabilities.* In general, a mutual fund distributes its gains to investors at the end of the year, and these gains are usually taxed as ordinary income. To avoid paying taxes on these distributions in the year of purchase, purchase mutual fund shares after they have occurred. Timing purchases in this way allows you to purchase more shares because the price of the fund shares will be reduced after distributions are made. Of course, these shares are worth less than before the distribution, but the total value remains the same.

You may reduce tax liabilities associated with the sale of mutual fund shares either by averaging the cost of all shares purchased when only a portion are sold or by specifying that the sale should include only the highest priced shares purchased on specific dates. In addition, many mutual fund investors purchase their shares through tax-exempt vehicles such as IRAs, 401ks, or Keogh plans.

How Does Time Affect Other Factors?

Time acts as a lens to either magnify or diminish the characteristics of risk, growth, income, and tax avoidance. Although time also influences the diversification and liquidity features of investments, these are, to a greater extent than the others, homogeneous across mutual funds, since every fund provides some level of diversification among companies, and mutual funds offer the promise of share redemption as the basis of liquidity. To understand the influence of time on decisions about your investment goals, it will simplify matters if these two aspects are set aside, as we consider how time interacts with risk, growth, income, and tax avoidance. For you to articulate your personal investment goals, it will be necessary to express them in relationship to time.

Risk. Typically, inflation over the past 10 years has averaged about 5 percent. In the next year there is very little risk of inflation exceeding 100 percent in the United States. There is a substantial risk of aggregate inflation exceeding 100 percent over the next 20 years because in 20 years, even at 5 percent per year, the aggregate will be 100 percent. However, the risk of loss with a sound investment in mutual funds or stocks made today is much more likely in the short term (next week or month) than over a long period, since the stock market has demonstrated a long-term trend of growth. Having a long enough investment horizon and being able to pick the time to sell will greatly reduce your risk of loss.

Growth. A $10,000 investment in one of the first mutual funds established in 1924 would be worth $30,000,000 today. A $10,000 investment in that same fund one week ago is probably still worth about $10,000, more or less.

Income. Zero-coupon bonds provide no income until their date of maturity. These bonds are purchased at a discount, and no interest is paid until maturity. However, one application of this investment is to provide additional income as an offset to college expenses during a limited time frame, by buying bonds which mature within the desired time period. If you buy bonds which mature during the years your children are in school, then the redemption of these bonds will provide money to finance their education. This is an example of appropriate matching of your liabilities (college expenses) with your assets (zero-coupon bonds of appropriate maturities).

Tax Avoidance. Although zero-coupon bonds provide no income during the period which precedes their maturity, they do not offer any measure of tax avoidance. Investors are obliged to declare "imputed" income on their tax returns, and pay taxes for each year this investment is held. There is no tax exemption or deferral during this time, except for zero-coupon municipal bonds, which are tax exempt.

One objective of this book is to provide you with guidance in assessing your tolerance for risk, needs for growth, income and tax avoidance. As we have seen in the preceding examples, these considerations have to be made specific to time periods in order to be sensible and to be a basis for investment decisions.

One example of how time is important is in its relationship to major life events, such as retirement or college expenses for your children. If you can plan far ahead for these events, you have an advantage over someone who has little time to plan ahead. Consider how you would make a general allocation of your investment assets in relation to the risks you are willing to take. As an illustration, refer to Figure 1-1, which has time in years on the horizontal (X) axis and risk level on the vertical (Y) axis.

The figure shows a goal of retirement income that will be required in about 20 years and relates this to low or moderate risk. As time passes, risk levels diminish because you are getting closer to your goal and need to take less risk.

Figure 1-1 demonstrates that the goal of a secure retirement income based on your investments does not necessarily require making investments which have low short-term risk characteristics. For example, an investment in good quality common stock which carries significant potential for short-term risk is very likely to appreciate significantly in a 20-year period. Therefore, this type of investment carries little long-term risk. So, such an investment is appropriate for the goal of retirement income. As you approach retirement, assets would be shifted toward investments in which short-term risk is lower in proportion to the diminishing time remaining. At the proposed retirement date all investments

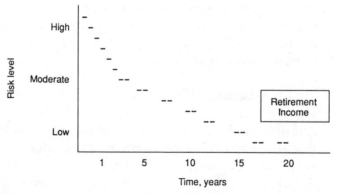

Figure 1-1. Retirement income goal and its relationship, over time, to risk.

would be low risk. Later on we will describe in depth how to use this approach to achieve your personal investment goals.

Assessing Your Financial Needs

To begin laying the foundations of the decision-making process, you will have to think over some of the basic financial needs you currently have and will have for the future.

Before you begin to assess your personal preferences and needs, let's take a quick look at the general financial needs people have. Although there are many categories, the most basic needs appear to be these seven:

Loss protection

Fund transferal

Cash access

Accumulation of wealth

Estate accumulation

Tax minimization

Credit

Loss Protection

"The Wheel of Fortune," a song of the early 1950s, was satirized by Mickey Katz in a Yiddish language version ("I'm a schlemiel of fortune") which included lyrics approximately as follows: "The wheel is turning, turning, turning. My heart is burning, burning, burning." Except for compulsive gamblers, no one likes to lose money. Most people want stability in their financial lives, at least to some degree, and need a financial basis they can count on. One means of obtaining this type of stability is to invest your money in secure, low-risk investments such as bank CDs or U.S. government securities. Another source of financial security might be earnings from a steady job or successful business. Many people believe home ownership contributes to financial security, and most responsible people pay for some forms of insurance which protect them against financial losses from health costs, liability, fire, theft, disability, and death. Your needs for loss protection will vary with actual and perceived financial responsibilities and the adequacy of your personal assets to meet those responsibilities in the event of misfortune.

Most financial experts recommend that home ownership, adequate insurance, and an emergency cash fund equivalent to several months of income precede investing. (See "Prerequisites to an Investment Program," later in this chapter.)

Fund Transferal

Through the remarkable achievements of computer technology, it is now possible to readily move funds among various accounts you might have with your bank or stockbroker. The purpose of these transfers is to maintain high balances in interest-bearing accounts until funds are moved into more accessible checking and credit card accounts to pay bills or make purchases. This way your money can be making money until you actually need it to cover checks.

Cash Access

Cash access needs are largely a matter of personal habits. If you usually carry thousands around with you, those needs can be satisfied simply by opening your wallet. But you also could lose your wallet. For many years, predating the automatic teller machine, a number of American Express customers "never carried more than $50.00 in cash." Although bank credit cards and other competitors to American Express have widely distributed their plastic alternatives to cash, it is astounding how frequently merchants and restaurants will decline to accept them. However, it is a surprisingly agreeable feeling to have $2.00 in your pocket 500 miles from home and to find a cash machine tied into a national ATM network that accepts your VISA card.

Accumulation of Wealth

Just as some people are tall and some are short, some thin and some fat, people differ in their needs for wealth accumulation. Many people live comfortably and happily within financial limits others would find oppressive, and many very wealthy people feel driven to acquire additional wealth. Most of us simply assume we want more money without asking ourselves how much would be enough, but if we thought about it, there probably is some limit to the amount of money we really want, especially once we have acquired the important things money can provide. So we need to think about how much we need to accumulate in order to set realistic goals for ourselves.

Estate Accumulation

The "need to bequeath" is probably the most open-ended feature of our desire to accumulate wealth, since it conveys to future generations financial benefits that are useless to you after interment. However, there is also a practical side to this matter—providing for the realistic needs of spouses and children who depend on you for financial support.

Tax Minimization

Although few people enjoy paying taxes, every person is not equal in terms of need to minimize taxes. For example, people earning less than $15,000 per year have far less need for tax minimization than people earning $100,000 per year. If your estate totals less than $600,000, its assets are exempt from federal estate taxes. If you already have significant tax reductions arising from sources such as home mortgage interest, your needs for tax minimization may be met to a sufficient extent that they are almost completely satisfied.

Credit

Credit has an effect on your investment program because good credit allows you to effectively manage your money and set aside part of your income and savings for this purpose. If you had no credit, you would have to pay cash for all your needs, such as a car or a house, and could not hope to carry out a plan for achieving investment goals.

You can be rich and not have good credit, and you can be poor and have great credit. Lenders are impressed by borrowers' past performance in borrowing and repaying sums of money. They make assumptions about you based on your credit history. So, if you have borrowed and repaid large sums promptly countless times in the past and have never defaulted on a loan, they are inclined to believe it is safe to lend you money even without any demonstration of your assets or income. Conversely, if you have no such history or, God forbid, the opposite is true and you are classified as a deadbeat, then you will need to prove your assets and income are security against a lender's risk even in borrowing rather small amounts. To some extent, your need for credit is associated with your creditworthiness, which is judged by past borrowing practices. When creditworthiness declines, credit needs increase and vice versa.

Retirement Funds

One of the problems with earning your way by being part of the "underground economy" (the part of the economy where few records are kept, payments are in cash, and taxes are ignored) is that you forgo the retirement benefits of the social security system at the same time as you avoid paying income taxes. The maximum amount of retirement income you can expect from social security at this time for a married couple (wife never employed) is about $16,000 annually. Many wage earners also have additional pension benefits provided by their employers and supplementary savings plans to which employers contribute. Estimates of income expected from these sources should be considered in calculating your needs for retirement.

Predictable Returns

If you are going to retire tomorrow morning and will rely on investment income to make up deficits between social security and pension benefits and lost wages, your need for predictable returns on your investments is high. However, if the anticipated retirement date is 20 years into the future, or if there is no deficit between current wages and expected benefits, you have much less need of predictable returns.

What are the Prerequisites to an Investment Program?

Certain conditions have to be met before you begin to allocate funds for investment. These fall into five major areas.

Insurance

To protect yourself and your dependents against financial losses from life's misfortunes, you need an adequate level of insurance against your death and against losses from fire, theft, and liabilities connected with your car and home and any businesses you own. Many people also have insurance against loss of income arising from disability or other misfortunes. To protect your family against financial loss arising from your death, you need to have adequate amounts of life insurance. These concerns are appropriate for discussion with property, casualty, and life insurance experts, who can advise you fully about them. In discussing life insurance, it is important to recognize that some forms of life insurance include an investment aspect and to separate the investment features of such insurance products from their death benefit protection in order to understand what you are buying when you pay your premiums.

Disposable Income

Disposable income is the income over which you have some discretion. In the investment context this means income which is not already committed for other items such as food, housing, debts, and other fundamental needs. At the beginning of Chapter 3 we provide worksheets for assessing net worth, net income, and net cash. The last two are directly related to disposable income. After you have completed that section you will know how much disposable income you have and will be able to decide how much of it you wish to set aside for investment.

There is a youthful segment of the U.S. population which is highly interested in and knowledgeable about investment activities but which holds little in the way of invested assets. These young people are at an early stage of their careers and do not have sufficient income to set aside for investment or have not had sufficient time to accumulate investment funds. When they reach an income that allows them to save, mutual fund investing can be an ideal method for them to participate in securities ownership through regular purchases of shares for small sums. Some employers have payroll deduction plans to assist employees who want to invest in this manner.

Emergency Fund

Liquid savings of at least several months' pay are adequate for most emergencies, especially if insurance coverage has been carefully worked out and credit is readily available through established credit lines and banking relationships. Six months' income is usually considered adequate, but if large expenses are anticipated you have to prepare for them in advance.

Housing

Since housing expenses are the most significant portion of after-tax expenditures for most people, and often a paramount need in terms of lifestyle requirements, the aspiring investor has to settle down in a cozy nest that he or she can afford before addressing investment concerns. The bag lady who lives in a cardboard box but keeps hundreds of thousands in savings accounts should not be a model to follow, but you might consider deferring consumption of luxurious housing in order to obtain funds for investment.

Access to Tax Advice

Although we discuss tax-advantaged investments in general terms in this book, this book is not intended to be a source for tax advice. Specific tax questions should be addressed to a qualified professional who can analyze your particular situation. A good, licensed accountant from whom you can get advice is essential in planning your investment strategy. In some complex cases, a tax attorney is also a necessary advisor. These experts will usually save you more in taxes than you expend on their fees. You will really appreciate their expertise if the IRS challenges your tax return.

Assessing Your Personal Preferences and Needs

Investment choices will result from several related factors:

1. Your inherent disposition to prefer high, moderate, or low levels of risk, growth, income, and tax avoidance
2. Your perceived financial needs and the priorities you assign to them
3. Your set of personal and financial circumstances
4. Incentives currently available in the financial markets

Personal and financial circumstances will be discussed in the next chapter, and marketplace incentives will be considered in subsequent chapters. In this section you will be able to gain insight into your preferences and financial priorities by participating in the following exercises:

- Trade-off analysis of investment preferences
- Priority ranking of current financial goals
- Time-money charting of ranked financial goals
- Quadrant analysis of investment prerequisites

Self-knowledge is both difficult to attain and highly valuable. Although the opportunity presented in this section is limited to the financial arena, it will offer prospects of some interesting "Aha!" experiences. For example, "Aha, I always suspected that I was afraid to take risks!" or "Aha, now I understand why growth is my highest priority!" You will also be amused to find that you are, or are not, as financially well prepared as you had thought. If you have ever consulted a financial planner, you will appreciate how the following self-assessment avoids the embarrassment which may accompany self-disclosure to a stranger. These exercises should provide a new awareness of financial aims, hopes, desires, and circumstances.

Trade-Off Analysis of Investment Preferences

In recent years, marketing researchers in academic and industry settings have developed a number of powerful techniques for evaluating consumers' preferences about products and services. One of these techniques, called "trade-off analysis," has been adapted here to help you determine your preferences in investment products.

This exercise asks you to indicate how likely you are to purchase investment products with various levels of the features that have been discussed in preceding sections. You are asked to respond to this question about nine different hypothetical products. Then, instructions are provided for you to analyze your own responses in order to quantify the influence of risk, growth potential, income potential, and tax avoidance on your purchase likelihood. As a result of this analysis, you will learn how powerful each of these factors is in shaping your choices, assuming all other dimensions (need priorities, circumstances, and incentive availability) are constant.

Questionnaire

Assume that you have $10,000 currently available to invest. Imagine that you are offered nine investments. For each investment, imagine how you would react to that particular investment as a place to invest your $10,000. Assume you are investing 100 percent of your available funds. For each of the nine investments described below, please rate your likelihood to purchase on the accompanying scale in which 0 represents "not at all likely" and 10 represents "very likely" to purchase. (*Note:* you should assume that each investment is evaluated on its own merit, as you perceive it, not as an alternative to the other eight investments. Therefore, rating an investment very highly does not reduce your ratings for the other investments. You could, conceivably, have multiple high ratings or multiple low ratings.)

1. *Investment A.* You will probably not lose any money by investing in this low-risk blue-chip security. Opportunities for growth and income are both high, although you will have to pay taxes fully on your gains and income. Please indicate how likely you are to purchase Investment A by circling the number which best represents your response:

0	1	2	3	4	5	6	7	8	9	10

Not at all   Somewhat   Very
likely to   likely to   likely to
purchase   purchase   purchase

2. *Investment B.* Although the market for this security is moderately risky, arising from unpredictable fluctuations in current and future values, experience shows that this security yields moderate growth and a low level of income. There are no tax avoidance features. Please indicate how likely you are to purchase Investment B by circling the number which best represents your response:

0	1	2	3	4	5	6	7	8	9	10

Not at all   Somewhat   Very
likely to   likely to   likely to
purchase   purchase   purchase

3. *Investment C.* By depositing your money in this no-risk government-insured account which is guaranteed to keep pace with inflation, you can be sure of moderate income coupled with low growth. There are no tax avoidance features. Please

indicate how likely you are to purchase Investment C by circling the number which best represents your response:

0	1	2	3	4	5	6	7	8	9	10

Not at all likely to purchase	Somewhat likely to purchase	Very likely to purchase

4. *Investment D.*   This zero-coupon municipal bond fund offers prospects for high growth and moderate levels of income through trading of issues which do not have high ratings and which are moderately risky. You could do very well with this investment, but in an economic downturn its value could decrease significantly. You will not pay federal income taxes on your gains or income. You will pay state and local taxes on this out-of-state fund. Please indicate how likely you are to purchase Investment D by circling the number which best represents your response:

0	1	2	3	4	5	6	7	8	9	10

Not at all likely to purchase	Somewhat likely to purchase	Very likely to purchase

5. *Investment E.*   Short-term U.S. Treasury bills, purchased at a discount, carry no risk, can provide high income and even moderate levels of growth. Interest is exempt from state and local taxes but is taxed as ordinary income at the federal level. Please indicate how likely you are to purchase Investment E by circling the number which best represents your response:

0	1	2	3	4	5	6	7	8	9	10

Not at all likely to purchase	Somewhat likely to purchase	Very likely to purchase

6. *Investment F.*   Although interest paid is low in comparison to competitive investment products and opportunities for capital growth are also rather low, U.S. savings bonds carry only a low long-term inflation risk and are exempt from state and local taxes. Federal income taxes are deferred until redemption. Please indicate how likely you are to purchase Investment F by circling the number which best represents your response:

0	1	2	3	4	5	6	7	8	9	10

Not at all likely to purchase	Somewhat likely to purchase	Very likely to purchase

7. *Investment G.* Assume your residence is in a city and state which enjoy very high ratings of their debt by the various rating services. No-risk zero-coupon bonds issued by your own municipality currently offer high growth, no current income, and complete exemption from federal, state, and local taxes. Please indicate how likely you are to purchase Investment G by circling the number which best represents your response:

0	1	2	3	4	5	6	7	8	9	10

Not at all likely to purchase	Somewhat likely to purchase	Very likely to purchase

8. *Investment H.* A variable deferred annuity is an investment with an insurance company that is low risk and can provide opportunities for moderate growth and income and high levels of tax avoidance. Please indicate how likely you are to purchase Investment H by circling the number which best represents your response:

0	1	2	3	4	5	6	7	8	9	10

Not at all likely to purchase	Somewhat likely to purchase	Very likely to purchase

9. *Investment I.* Distressed residential rental properties can offer high income coupled with high levels of tax avoidance, if you manage the property wisely. There is always a moderate risk with this type of investment, and growth may be relatively low over time. Please indicate how likely you are to purchase Investment I by circling the number which best represents your response:

0	1	2	3	4	5	6	7	8	9	10

Not at all likely to purchase	Somewhat likely to purchase	Very likely to purchase

Record your responses on the following worksheet:

Answer Sheet

Investment	*Score*
A	_____
B	_____
C	_____
D	_____
E	_____
F	_____
G	_____
H	_____
I	_____
Total score:	_____
Total score divided by 9:	_____

(This is the average of your likelihood ratings.)

Analyzing Your Responses

The following instructions are provided for you to analyze your own responses in order to quantify the influence of risk, growth, income, and tax avoidance on your purchase likelihood. As a result of this analysis, you will learn how powerful each of these factors is in shaping your choices, assuming all other dimensions (need priorities, circumstances, and incentive availability) are constant.

To begin the analysis of your questionnaire responses, simply take the average of your likelihood ratings for the nine investments which you computed on the worksheet and record that number below.

1. Overall average likelihood rating: _____

Risk
To find the contribution risk levels make to your likelihood rating, proceed as follows:

1. Add the likelihood ratings for Investment C, Investment E, and Investment G. Divide by 3 and record below.

    Likelihood rating for Investment C: _____

    Likelihood rating for Investment E: _____

    Likelihood rating for Investment G: _____

    Total _____ ÷ 3 = _____

    No-risk average likelihood rating: _____

    Subtract the overall average from the no-risk average to find the unique contribution of the no-risk level, called the "no-risk part worth," and record below.

    No-risk part worth: _____

2. Add the likelihood ratings for Investment A, Investment F, and Investment H. Divide by 3 and record below.

    Likelihood rating for Investment A: _____

    Likelihood rating for Investment F: _____

    Likelihood rating for Investment H: _____

    Total _____ ÷ 3 = _____

    Low-risk average likelihood rating: _____

    Subtract the overall average from the low-risk average to find the unique contribution of the low-risk level, called the "low-risk part worth," and record below.

    Low-risk part worth: _____

3. Add the likelihood ratings for Investment B, Investment D, and Investment I. Divide by 3 and record below.

    Likelihood rating for Investment B: _____

    Likelihood rating for Investment D: _____

    Likelihood rating for Investment I: _____

    Total _____ ÷ 3 = _____

    Moderate-risk average likelihood rating: _____

    Subtract the overall average from the moderate-risk average to find the unique contribution of the moderate-risk level and record below.

    Moderate-risk part worth: _____

To understand what this analysis reveals about your preferences for risk levels you need to realize that the part worths represent either additions to or subtractions from your likelihood to purchase. For example, if the part worth for moderate risk is 1.50, then it adds 1.5 scale points to your likelihood to purchase when you are confronted with a moderate risk investment, all other factors being equal. However, this value could be negative and would then represent a reduction of purchase likelihood. You also would want to consider how the levels compare to each other and whether there is a meaningful pattern in the direction and magnitude of part worths associated with risk level. Finally, what is the range among these part worths? Subtract the lowest value from the highest and record below.

4.   Range of risk part worths: _____

Growth
To find the contribution growth levels make to your likelihood ratings, continue the analysis as follows:

1.   Add the likelihood ratings for Investment C, Investment F, and Investment I. Divide by 3 and record below.

   Likelihood rating for Investment C: _____

   Likelihood rating for Investment F: _____

   Likelihood rating for Investment I: _____

   Total _____ ÷ 3 = _____

Low-growth average likelihood rating: _____

Subtract the overall average from the low-growth average to find the unique contribution of the low-growth level and record below.

Low-growth part worth: _____

2.   Add the likelihood ratings for Investment B, Investment E, and Investment H. Divide by 3 and record below.

   Likelihood rating for Investment B: _____

   Likelihood rating for Investment E: _____

   Likelihood rating for Investment H: _____

   Total _____ ÷ 3 = _____

Moderate-growth average likelihood rating: _____

Subtract the overall average from the moderate-growth average to find the unique contribution of the moderate-growth level and record below.

Moderate-growth part worth: _____

3. Add the likelihood ratings for Investment A, Investment D, and Investment G. Divide by 3 and record below.

Likelihood rating for Investment A: _____

Likelihood rating for Investment D: _____

Likelihood rating for Investment G: _____

Total _____ ÷ 3 = _____

High-growth average likelihood rating: _____

Subtract the overall average from the high-growth average to find the unique contribution of the high-growth level and record below.

High-growth part worth: _____

Interpret the part worths for growth levels exactly as you did for risk. The part worths either add to or subtract from your likelihood to purchase. Compare part worths and look for a meaningful pattern. Subtract the lowest value from the highest and record below.

4. Range of growth part worths: _____

Income
Continue the analysis by finding the contribution income levels make to your likelihood ratings.

1. Add the likelihood ratings for Investment B, Investment F, and Investment G. Divide by 3 and record below.

Likelihood rating for Investment B: _____

Likelihood rating for Investment F: _____

Likelihood rating for Investment G: _____

Total _____ ÷ 3 = _____

Low-income average likelihood rating: _____

Subtract the overall average from the low-income average to find the unique contribution of the low-income level and record below.

Low-income part worth: _____

2. Add the likelihood ratings for Investment C, Investment D, and Investment H. Divide by 3 and record below.

Likelihood rating for Investment C: _____

Likelihood rating for Investment D: _____

Likelihood rating for Investment H: _____

Total _____ ÷ 3 = _____

Moderate-income likelihood rating: _____

Subtract the overall average from the moderate-income average to find the unique contribution of the moderate-income level and record below.

Moderate-income part worth: _____

3. Add the likelihood ratings for Investment A, Investment E, and Investment I. Divide by 3 and record below.

    Likelihood rating for Investment A: _____

    Likelihood rating for Investment E: _____

    Likelihood rating for Investment I: _____

    Total _____ ÷ 3 = _____

High-income likelihood rating: _____

Subtract the overall average from the high-income average to find the unique contribution of the high-income level and record below.

High-income part worth: _____

Interpret part worths for income exactly as you did for risk and growth. Look for a meaningful pattern. Subtract the lowest value from the highest and record below.

4. Range of income part worths: _____

Tax Avoidance
Complete the last subsection of the analysis by finding how tax avoidance contributes to your likelihood ratings.

1. Add the likelihood ratings for Investment A, Investment B, and Investment C. Divide by 3 and record below.

    Likelihood rating for Investment A: _____

    Likelihood rating for Investment B: _____

    Likelihood rating for Investment C: _____

    Total _____ ÷ 3 = _____

No-tax-avoidance average likelihood rating: _____

Subtract the overall average from the no-tax-avoidance average to find the unique contribution of the no-tax-avoidance level and record below.

No-tax-avoidance part worth: _____

2. Add the likelihood ratings for Investment D, Investment E, and Investment F. Divide by 3 and record below.

   Likelihood rating for Investment D: _____

   Likelihood rating for Investment E: _____

   Likelihood rating for Investment F: _____

   Total _____ ÷ 3 = _____

   Moderate-tax-avoidance likelihood rating: _____

   Subtract the overall average from the moderate-tax-avoidance average to find the unique contribution of the moderate-tax-avoidance level and record below.

   Moderate-tax-avoidance part worth: _____

3. Add the likelihood ratings for Investment G, Investment H, and Investment I. Divide by 3 and record below.

   Likelihood rating for Investment G: _____

   Likelihood rating for Investment H: _____

   Likelihood rating for Investment I: _____

   Total _____ ÷ 3 = _____

   High-tax-avoidance average likelihood rating: _____

   Subtract the overall average from the high-tax-avoidance average to find the unique contribution of the high-tax-avoidance level and record below.

   High-tax-avoidance part worth: _____

Complete your interpretation of the effects financial characteristics have on your likelihood to purchase investment products by examining the pattern found in tax avoidance part worths. Subtract the lowest value from the highest and record below.

4. Range of tax avoidance part worths: _____

Importance of Investment Features

The analysis and interpretation you just conducted should provide insight into the influence various levels of investment characteristics have on your preferences for investment products. By examining the ranges you can develop a rank ordering of the importance of these investment features. The trade-off analysis allows you to rank the importance of investment characteristics simply by assigning a 1 to the characteristic that has the highest range, a 2 to the next highest range, etc. Please record the rankings in the following box:

Summary of Investment Characteristic Rankings

Most important investment feature: _____

Second most important investment feature: _____

Third most important feature: _____

Least important investment feature: _____

How Desirable Is Each Investment Feature Level?

To assign rankings to the part worths of each investment characteristic, for each characteristic assign a 1 to the most positive (or least negative) level, assign a 2 to the second most positive (or least negative) level, and assign a 3 to the third most positive (or least negative) level. Record part worth rankings in the following box:

Summary of Part Worths Rankings

	No	Low	Moderate	High
Risk	_____	_____	_____	
Growth		_____	_____	_____
Income		_____	_____	_____
Tax avoidance	_____		_____	_____

Priority Ranking of Current Financial Goals

Earlier in this chapter we listed some general financial needs. In this exercise you will review a checklist designed to help you specify your future goals. First, review the list and check those items which represent goals you now have or expect to have. Then, rank your top five by putting a 1 next to the goal which describes the highest priority, a 2 next to the second highest priority, and so on. If you have financial goals that are not listed here, please enter them in the spaces to the right and rank them as well.

Rank	Financial Goal	Rank	Financial Goal
_____	Retirement income	_____	_____
_____	Accumulating an estate	_____	_____
_____	Buying a house	_____	_____
_____	Buying a car	_____	_____
_____	Children's education	_____	_____
_____	Expensive vacation	_____	_____
_____	Financial independence	_____	_____
_____	Paying off debt	_____	_____
_____	Current income	_____	_____
_____	Daughter's wedding	_____	_____
_____	Accumulating wealth	_____	_____

Financial Goal Time-Money Requirements

As discussed earlier, financial goals need to be expressed together with the time frame in which they are to be accomplished. To get a clearer picture of your objectives, record below the top five ranked financial goals you have selected in the previous section. Then indicate in the next column to the right the time frame for these goals (e.g., 10 years from now, immediately, 2001 to 2010). In the column to the far right state the amount of money you will need for each goal (e.g., $50 per month, $10,000, $10,000,000):

	Financial Goal	Time Frame	Amount Required
1.	_____	_____	$_____
2.	_____	_____	$_____
3.	_____	_____	$_____
4.	_____	_____	$_____
5.	_____	_____	$_____

Finding Your Unfulfilled Financial Needs (Quadrant Analysis)

Another technique that has been developed by researchers for understanding the attitudes of consumers is called "quadrant analysis." In quadrant analysis you demonstrate which important financial needs are not being adequately met.

How well you are handling the prerequisites to investing can be readily demonstrated in the following exercise. For each item in the following list, record your judgment of the importance of each prerequisite in maintaining your peace of mind. Use the following rating scale to judge importance:

1 = Not at all important

2 = Not too important

3 = Fairly important

4 = Very important

5 = Extremely important

Prerequisite	*Importance Rating*
Insurance	
Life	_____
Health	_____
Property, casualty	_____
Liability	_____
Other	_____
Disposable income	_____
Emergency fund	_____
Housing	_____
Access to tax advice	_____

In the next step of this analysis, consider how adequately you have currently fulfilled these prerequisites. Rate each item on the following scale for adequacy:

1 = Not at all adequate

2 = Not too adequate

3 = Fairly adequate

4 = Very adequate

5 = Extremely adequate

Prerequisite	Adequacy Rating
Insurance	
Life	_____
Health	_____
Property, casualty	_____
Liability	_____
Other	_____
Disposable income	_____
Emergency fund	_____
Housing	_____
Access to tax advice	_____

In Figure 1-2 use the X axis to represent adequacy and the Y axis to represent importance. Plot each prerequisite using the ratings you have just made as coordinates. For example, if life insurance was rated 3 on the adequacy scale and 4 on the importance scale, it would be represented by the circle already drawn on the chart. The origin (where the axes meet) is a 3 on both rating scales.

Note those items in the upper left quadrant. These are high in importance and low in adequacy and therefore require your attention before you proceed with any of your investment priorities.

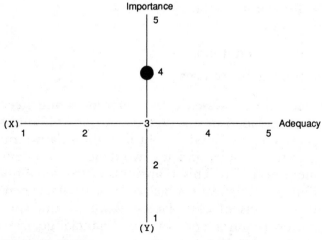

Figure 1-2. Plot your prerequisites to determine your financial needs.

Chapter Summary

You will recall there are six main features of investment plans. Two of these, liquidity and diversification, are to some extent the same for most mutual funds. The other four—risk, growth, income, and tax avoidance—have to be considered in relation to time to be meaningful. There are five prerequisites to an investment program:

- Insurance
- Disposable income
- Emergency fund
- Housing
- Access to tax advice

Broadly, people have a limited number of financial needs:

Loss protection

Fund transferal

Cash access

Wealth accumulation

Estate accumulation

Tax minimization

Credit

Retirement funds

Predictable returns

You have assessed your preferences and needs in three exercises included in this chapter. A trade-off analysis of investment preferences offered insight into the relative importance of risk, growth, income, and tax avoidance in influencing your investment decisions. This analysis also provided a quantitative evaluation of the appeal (or lack of appeal) associated with each of the three levels of each factor. Ranking and specifying time and money requirements for your financial goals allowed you to appreciate exactly what your own objectives and priorities are. Finally, an assessment based on your own judgments of importance and adequacy of fulfillment points out prerequisites to an investment program which need your attention.

2
Long-Term Plans

In this chapter you will consider your long-term plans and assess your current financial situation. Then we provide an illustration presented in a story format of how to use the concepts.

What Are Your Long-Term Plans?

Peoples' financial needs can be summarized using two words—*protection* and *accumulation*. Most of the transactions engaged in, and most requests for assistance, serve these two important functions. Numerous factors influence the satisfaction of these needs apart from individual preferences and dispositions. These factors are largely situational and change as a person's circumstances change. In this chapter you will find guidance for evaluating what kind of investor you should be, taking into account age, marital status, dependents, income, and assets.

These circumstantial influences on financial decisions interact with knowledge, willingness to accept risk, liquidity requirements, and investment experience at various stages of life. By considering the current phase of your "financial life-space" and comparing it to desired future phases, you will get the insight you need into the choices necessary to travel along a path that seems right for you.

Assessment of Current Financial Situation

One way of thinking about your financial situation is to regard yourself as a business. In the business world corporate entities review their financial status in annual statements; in these statements, accountants capture three major categories of information:

1. Net worth = assets − liabilities
2. Net income = gross income − expenses
3. Net cash = cash available to invest or spend

These same categories also apply to individuals. If you want a concise yet comprehensive picture of your own current financial status, construct your own personal financial review by completing the balance sheet, income statement, and cash flow statement in Figures 2-1, 2-2, and 2-3.

When you have established your current assessment on net worth, net income, and net cash, you can appreciate where you stand financially in much the same way as you would understand the financial position of a business enterprise. Just as a business executive would, before making any investment decisions carefully think over short- and long-term goals that are appropriate to your plans and the current economic environment (which may favor one or another type of investment strategy).

How to Make Long-Range Plans

Age

The first question to address in constructing a long-term investment plan is "What is the duration of my plan?" Age is the most critical factor to consider. At age 70 your current life expectancy is about 12 years if you are a man, 15 years if you are a woman. You may think it prudent to think about 20 years (if you are an optimist, if not, perhaps 20 minutes), but planning of greater than 20 years' duration is probably not called for. At age 30, however, thinking ahead as far as 50 years would not be excessive.

Balance Sheet

Today's Date _____

Assets

  Cash or liquid investments   _____

  Short-term investments   _____

  Receivables (money owed to you)   _____

  Personal property   _____

  Real estate   _____

  Current value of

     1. Retirement funds   _____

     2. Business equity   _____

     3. Collectibles   _____

     4. Expected inheritance   _____

  Other   _____

    Total assets   _____

Liabilities and net worth

  Mortgages   _____

  Personal loans   _____

  Credit card balances   _____

  Unpaid taxes   _____

  Other debts payable   _____

    Total liabilities

Total net worth (assets − liabilities)   _____

Figure 2-1. Balance sheet.

Statement of Income

Today's Date _____

Income
  Earned income
    Salaries .... _____

    Business income .... _____

  Investment income .... _____

  Other income (Social Security,
    retirement, insurance reimbursement) ...... _____

Total gross income .... _____

Expenses

Taxes
  Taxes on income .... _____

  Real estate taxes .... _____

  Sales taxes .... _____

  Other taxes .... _____

Total tax expense .... _____

Household expenses
  Rent or mortgage payment .... _____

  Utilities/heating .... _____

  Repairs .... _____

  Insurance .... _____

Figure 2-2. Income statement.

Automobile expenses

   Lease or loan payments   _____

   Fuel   _____

   Maintenance   _____

   Repairs   _____

   Insurance   _____

Family expenses

   Support of self, spouse, and children
     (clothing, food, etc.)   _____

   Medical insurance   _____

   Child care   _____

   Current educational expenses   _____

Entertainment

   Restaurants   _____

   Home entertainment (VCRs, audio
     and videotapes, etc.)   _____

   Films, theater, concerts   _____

   Other   _____

All other miscellaneous expenses   _____

Total expenses   _____

Total net income (income − expenses)   _____

Figure 2-2. (*Continued*)

Cash Flow Analysis

Today's Date _____

Cash available

  Cash and liquid investments (current)   _____

  Cash and liquid investments receivable
    within the next 12 months   _____

  Available credit (current)   _____

  Available credit readily obtainable within
    the next 12 months   _____

  Total cash available within next
    12 months   _____

Cash obligations

  Fixed obligations next 12 months

    Interest payments (current)

      Mortgage   _____

      Auto loan   _____

      Credit cards   _____

      Other debt   _____

  Total current interest payments   _____

    Principle payments (current)

      Mortgage   _____

      Auto loan   _____

      Credit cards   _____

      Other debt   _____

Figure 2-3. Cash flow analysis.

Total current principle payments   _____

   Taxes to be paid (next 12 months)   _____

   Other fixed obligations (next 12 months)   _____

    Total fixed obligations (next 12 months)   _____

Disposable cash flow

   Total cash available minus total fixed
   obligations   _____

Net disposable cash flow   _____

1. Disposable cash flow minus additional
    payments to interest and principal
    for available credit used during
    next 12 months   _____

2. Disposable cash flow minus projected
    cash paid for nonfixed expenses during
    next 12 months   _____

Your goal for cash available 12 months
    from today   _____

Net cash (available next 12 months)   _____

   Net disposable cash flow – your goals
   for cash available in 12 months   _____

Figure 2-3. (*Continued*)

Stages of Life

Although age is a major determinant of where a person stands in the human life cycle, there is a great deal of flexibility in lifestyle choices people can make at any age. These choices may include unusual family and dependent arrangements that are not synchronous with the customary or conventional choices made in this area. For example, a man of 50 might marry a 30-year-old woman and become a father at an age when other men are grandfathers. The range of possibilities includes a large number of combinations associated with marital, family dependent, and employment status (retired, preretired, employed, unemployed) and becomes quite complex when you add varying degrees of income and wealth. Rather than present a voluminous and comprehensive treatment of this subject, which would not offer practical guidance to you in making future plans, the next section offers a simplified method that will help you assess where you are now and where you expect to be, or hope to be, at various points in the future.

Creating a Plan

First, choose a time frame, for example, 40 years, based on your current age (see Table 2-1), and enter some critical life events anticipated on the continuum for your life. An example of a life continuum is given first:

Example of Life Continuum

Time:	Present	3 yrs	10 yrs	12 yrs	15 yrs	17 yrs	20 yrs	25 yrs	30 yrs	40 yrs	from now
Critical events:	Age 40	Purchase house	First child enters college	Second child enters college	First child finishes college	Second child finishes college	Parent's leave inheritance by now	Retirement	Sell house	Death	

Your Life Continuum

Time:	Present										
Critical events:	Age								Death		

Table 2-1. Expectation of U.S. Life and Mortality Rates at Single Years of Age by Race and Sex, 1987

	Expectation of life (years)					Mortality rate per 1000				
	Total per-sons	White		All other		Total per-sons	White		All other	
Age		Male	Female	Male	Female		Male	Female	Male	Female
0	75.0	72.2	78.9	67.3	75.2	101.1	9.6	7.6	17.0	14.0
1	74.7	71.9	78.5	67.4	75.3	.7	.7	.6	1.1	.8
2	73.8	71.0	77.6	66.5	74.3	.5	.5	.4	.8	.7
3	72.8	70.0	76.6	65.6	73.4	.4	.4	.3	.7	.6
4	71.9	69.0	75.6	64.6	72.4	.4	.4	.3	.6	.4
5	70.9	68.1	74.7	63.6	71.4	.3	.3	.2	.5	.4
6	69.9	67.1	73.7	62.7	70.5	.3	.3	.2	.4	.3
7	68.9	66.1	72.7	61.7	69.5	.2	.3	.2	.4	.3
8	67.9	65.1	71.7	60.7	68.5	.2	.3	.2	.3	.2
9	66.9	64.1	70.7	59.7	67.5	.2	.2	.1	.3	.2
10	66.0	63.1	69.7	58.8	66.5	.2	.2	.1	.3	.2
11	65.0	62.2	68.7	57.8	65.5	.2	.2	.1	.3	.2
12	64.0	61.2	67.7	56.8	64.6	.2	.3	.2	.4	.2
13	63.0	60.2	66.8	55.8	63.6	.3	.4	.2	.5	.2
14	62.0	59.2	65.8	54.8	62.6	.5	.6	.3	.7	.3
15	61.0	58.2	64.8	53.9	61.6	.6	.8	.4	.9	.3
16	60.1	57.3	63.8	52.9	60.6	.8	1.0	.5	1.1	.4
17	59.1	56.4	62.8	52.0	59.6	.9	1.2	.5	1.3	.5
18	58.2	55.4	61.9	51.0	58.7	1.0	1.3	.5	1.6	.5
19	57.2	54.5	60.9	50.1	57.7	1.0	1.4	.5	1.8	.6
20	56.3	53.6	59.9	49.2	56.7	1.1	1.5	.5	2.1	.7
21	55.3	52.6	59.0	48.3	55.8	1.1	1.6	.5	2.3	.8
22	54.4	51.7	58.0	47.4	54.8	1.2	1.6	.5	2.5	.8
23	53.5	50.8	57.0	46.5	53.9	1.2	1.6	.5	2.6	.9
24	52.5	49.9	56.1	45.7	52.9	1.2	1.6	.5	2.7	.9
25	51.6	49.0	55.1	44.8	52.0	1.2	1.6	.5	2.7	.9
26	50.7	48.0	54.1	43.9	51.0	1.2	1.5	.6	2.7	1.0
27	49.7	47.1	53.1	43.0	50.0	1.2	1.5	.6	2.8	1.0
28	48.8	46.2	52.2	42.1	49.1	1.2	1.6	.6	3.0	1.1
29	47.8	45.3	51.2	41.3	48.2	1.3	1.6	.6	3.2	1.2

Table 2-1. Expectation of U.S. Life and Mortality Rates at Single Years of Age by Race and Sex, 1987 (*Continued*)

	Expectation of life (years)					Mortality rate per 1000				
	Total per-sons	White		All other		Total per-sons	White		All other	
Age		Male	Female	Male	Female		Male	Female	Male	Female
30	46.9	44.3	50.2	40.4	47.2	1.3	1.7	.6	3.4	1.3
31	46.0	43.4	49.3	39.5	46.3	1.4	1.7	.7	3.6	1.5
32	45.0	42.5	48.3	38.7	45.3	1.5	1.8	.7	3.8	1.6
33	44.1	41.6	47.3	37.8	44.4	1.5	1.9	.7	4.0	1.7
34	43.1	40.6	46.4	37.0	43.5	1.6	1.9	.8	4.3	1.8
35	42.2	39.7	45.4	36.1	42.6	1.7	2.0	.8	4.6	1.9
36	41.3	38.8	44.4	35.3	41.6	1.8	2.1	.9	4.9	2.0
37	40.4	37.9	43.5	34.5	40.7	1.9	2.2	1.0	5.2	2.1
38	39.4	37.0	42.5	33.6	39.8	2.0	2.3	1.0	5.5	2.2
39	38.5	36.0	41.6	32.8	38.9	2.1	2.4	1.1	5.7	2.4
40	37.6	35.1	40.6	32.0	38.0	2.2	2.5	1.2	5.9	2.6
41	36.7	34.2	39.7	31.2	37.1	2.3	2.7	1.3	6.2	2.8
42	35.8	33.3	38.7	30.4	36.2	2.4	2.8	1.4	6.4	3.0
43	34.8	32.4	37.8	29.6	35.3	2.6	3.1	1.6	6.8	3.2
44	33.9	31.5	36.8	28.8	34.4	2.9	3.3	1.8	7.1	3.5
45	33.0	30.6	35.9	28.0	33.5	3.2	3.6	2.0	7.5	3.7
46	32.1	29.7	35.0	27.2	32.6	3.5	4.0	2.2	7.9	4.0
47	31.2	28.8	34.0	26.4	31.8	3.8	4.4	2.5	8.5	4.3
48	30.4	27.9	33.1	25.6	30.9	4.2	4.8	2.7	9.2	4.8
49	29.5	27.1	32.2	24.9	30.1	4.6	5.4	3.0	10.0	5.3
50	28.6	26.2	31.3	24.1	29.2	5.1	6.0	3.4	11.0	5.8
51	27.8	25.4	30.4	23.4	28.4	5.7	6.6	3.7	12.0	6.4
52	26.9	24.5	29.5	22.6	27.6	6.2	7.3	4.1	12.9	7.0
53	26.1	23.7	28.6	21.9	26.7	6.8	8.1	4.5	13.7	7.5
54	25.3	22.9	27.8	21.2	25.9	7.4	9.0	4.9	14.5	8.0
55	24.4	22.1	26.9	20.5	25.2	8.0	9.8	5.3	15.3	8.5
56	23.6	21.3	26.0	19.8	24.4	8.7	10.7	5.8	16.2	9.0
57	22.8	20.5	25.2	19.2	23.6	9.5	11.8	6.4	17.4	9.8
58	22.1	19.8	24.3	18.5	22.8	10.5	13.1	7.1	18.8	10.7

Table 2-1. Expectation of U.S. Life and Mortality Rates at Single Years of Age by Race and Sex, 1987 (*Continued*)

	Expectation of life (years)					Mortality rate per 1000				
	Total per-sons	White		All other		Total per-sons	White		All other	
Age		Male	Female	Male	Female		Male	Female	Male	Female
59	21.3	19.0	23.5	17.8	22.1	11.6	14.4	7.8	20.5	11.9
60	20.5	18.3	22.7	17.2	21.3	12.7	16.0	8.6	22.4	13.2
61	19.8	17.6	21.9	16.6	20.6	14.0	17.6	9.5	24.4	14.5
62	19.1	16.9	21.1	16.0	19.9	15.2	19.2	10.4	26.3	15.7
63	18.3	16.2	20.3	15.4	19.2	16.4	20.7	11.3	28.0	16.7
64	17.6	15.6	19.5	14.8	18.5	17.6	22.2	12.3	29.7	17.6
65	16.9	14.9	18.8	14.3	17.8	18.8	23.8	13.3	31.3	18.6
66	16.3	14.3	18.0	13.7	17.2	20.2	25.5	14.4	33.2	19.6
67	15.6	13.6	17.3	13.2	16.5	21.8	27.7	15.7	35.3	20.9
68	14.9	13.0	16.5	12.6	15.8	23.8	30.3	17.1	37.8	22.6
69	14.3	12.4	15.8	12.1	15.2	26.0	33.5	18.8	40.6	24.6
70	13.6	11.8	15.1	11.6	14.6	28.5	36.9	20.6	43.7	26.8
71	13.0	11.2	14.4	11.1	13.9	31.1	40.6	22.6	47.0	29.1
72	12.4	10.7	13.7	10.6	13.3	33.8	44.4	24.7	50.0	31.4
73	11.9	10.2	13.1	10.2	12.8	36.6	48.3	27.0	53.6	33.4
74	11.3	9.6	12.4	9.7	12.2	39.6	52.4	29.5	56.8	35.4
75	10.7	9.1	11.8	9.3	11.6	42.8	56.7	32.3	60.0	37.6
76	10.2	8.7	11.2	8.8	11.1	46.3	61.5	35.4	63.9	40.1
77	9.7	8.2	10.6	8.4	10.5	50.2	66.7	38.9	68.3	43.3
78	9.1	7.8	10.0	8.0	10.0	54.7	72.6	42.9	73.5	47.2
79	8.6	7.3	9.4	7.6	9.4	59.6	79.1	47.4	79.6	52.0
80	8.2	6.9	8.8	7.2	8.9	65.3	86.2	52.5	86.8	57.7
81	7.7	6.5	8.3	6.9	8.4	71.6	94.1	58.4	95.1	64.6
82	7.2	6.1	7.8	6.5	8.0	78.9	102.6	65.3	104.9	72.7
83	6.8	5.8	7.3	6.2	7.6	87.1	111.8	73.3	116.3	82.3
84	6.4	5.5	6.8	6.0	7.2	96.5	121.4	83.0	129.8	93.8
85	6.1	5.2	6.4	5.8	6.9					

SOURCE: National Center for Health Statistics. *Vital Statistics of the United States, 1987*; vol. II, sec. 6, Life Tables, DHHS publication no. (PHS) 90-1104.

The five important financial goals which you set for yourself at the end of Chapter 2 should be represented on this continuum by their associated life events. In addition, other financial goals which may be less important because of their remoteness in time and other life events (with or without clear financial implications) may be anticipated here. For example, you may expect to come into an inheritance at a particular time in the future, or you may intend at 60 years old to go to law school or to enter a monastery in Tibet. The lifelong perspective you take in examining your desires and expectations for the future will help you avoid tunnel vision in your short-term planning.

Planning for Change as Life Evolves

What other people are you most like, and do their financial needs resemble your own? As time goes on and your circumstances change to be more similar to those of other "clusters" of people, your financial needs will also change. Perhaps today you are a single young adult earning $20,000 per year and living in a shared apartment with other young men or women. Your financial needs and goals today are vastly different from what they will be 20 years from now if you are married, solidly middle-aged, earning $50,000 per year, struggling with mortgage and car payments, with teenaged children approaching their college years. Shouldn't your financial plans take account of this future status if you expect to be in similar circumstances some day? If you were looking backward from the vantage point of the future, would you wish that you had planned ahead? Why not make that wish come true?

Perhaps it is too early in your plan to take action to prepare for events that are remote, but you can still recognize that those events will occur and set a tentative date to begin preparing for them. To return to the example of a life continuum, the retirement date established was 25 years in the future. You might not want to attend to planning for retirement now but simply to determine that 5 years from now you will begin to prepare for that remote event. If you allow for this type of planning deferral as part of your long-range plan, you can map out a lifetime financial strategy that does not have to be all-inclusive at the start.

All people are unique individuals with special needs and desires, but we can gain some insight and objectivity about ourselves by comparing our own circumstances to those of others whom we might resemble. Listed below are six descriptions based on clusters of social-demographic characteristics found in recent U.S. census data. Each description represents a major segment of the U.S. population in terms of age, income, assets, and family and marital status. Please examine these descriptions carefully. The next step in your journey toward financial fulfillment is to identify one of these descriptions which most closely resembles your current situation. Perhaps it may be necessary to blend two of them in your mind in order to adequately represent your circumstances. Read these descriptions now and decide which one or two are most similar to your own set of situational attributes. Then go on to the next section.

Wealthy Families.   These families have substantial assets and high incomes. Parents are in their middle years, are well educated, and work in the professions, in management, or in sales. There are usually one or two school-aged children. These families own expensive homes, have high net worth and high discretionary income.

Moderately Well-off Families.   The largest grouping of households is in this category. These families have average income and some assets, primarily equity in their own homes. Parents may or may not have college degrees, work in skilled or semiskilled occupations or for the military. Although there is a broad range of ages in this group, children tend to be of elementary school age.

Poor Families.   These families have no assets worth mentioning and have low incomes. Parents are poorly educated and work in unskilled jobs. There are usually three or more children. These families rent their homes and have either poor credit or high credit card debt.

Younger Singles.   Unmarried people living alone who tend to have average or above-average incomes are in this category. Many have graduated from college and work in professional, managerial, or sales positions. They rent their homes and do not have high levels of assets, but their credit is good.

Younger Couples.   Married, childless people who are on their way toward achieving a "family" household status, or married couples who do not expect to have children, may fall in a broad range of income and educational categories. Most do not have substantial accumulated assets and rent their homes.

Seniors.   Seniors are 65 years of age or older and are either retired or approaching retirement. Most households consist of older married couples or widows. Most seniors own their own homes, have average or below-average income and some assets with little or no debt.

Transitions

Now that you have decided which cluster best represents your current situation, refer to the diagram you completed earlier: "Your Life Continuum." What is the first life event which has financial significance? Do you hope or desire that your circumstances at the time of the occurrence of the projected event will be different than they are now? Will you be, or hope to be, associated with different cluster descriptions when the event occurs? Please consider succeeding life events listed on "Your Life Continuum" and record in the following checklist the anticipated cluster descriptions you expect to, or hope to, resemble at the time each life event occurs:

Life Events	*Anticipated Cluster*
1. Present	1. _____
2. _____	2. _____
3. _____	3. _____
4. _____	4. _____
5. _____	5. _____
6. _____	6. _____
7. _____	7. _____

Now you already know something about the specific financial goals you will need to reach to prepare for these expected life events, and you also have made judgments about the expected context and circumstances you will be in as they occur. There are implied changes, from one condition to another over time, which you expect to happen or hope will occur. To consider these objectively, you might look at these changes as *transitions* which another person, your "friend," will undergo and offer your best financial advice in the following exercise.

To achieve the *first transition,* which factors would you most strongly advise to have the greatest influence upon your "friend's" financial decisions? Rank them in order in the following checklist, the most important (1) to the least important (4).

Factors	Rank
Risk	_____
Growth	_____
Income	_____
Tax avoidance	_____

With reference to the *first transition,* which levels of each of the following factors would be most appropriate and which least appropriate in choosing trade-offs in an investment portfolio suitable to accomplish the required change? Rank the levels from most appropriate choices (first) to least appropriate (third) for each of the following:

First Transition: Choice Rankings

	No	Low	Moderate	High
Risk	____	____	____	
Growth		____	____	____
Income		____	____	____
Tax avoidance	____		____	____

Compared to the preference rankings of investment characteristics developed in Chapter 1, are the rankings you found in the preceding exercise the same or different? If they are different, you will need to decide on a final judgment of how to handle your "friend's" investments for the *first transition* which reconciles preferences with needs. Record that judgment:

First Transition	
Investment Factor	*Final Importance Rank*
Risk	_____
Growth	_____
Income	_____
Tax avoidance	_____

When you computed part worths for each level of the factors considered at the end of the previous chapter, you found values for each level that were first, second, and third in terms of their positive contribution to likelihood of purchase. Compare these implicit rankings to the explicit rankings found above. Are they the same or different? If they are different, carefully reconsider and reconcile them, and record below your final judgment of your "friend's" best choice of levels for each investment factor to achieve the *first transition:*

First Transition: Final Level Rankings			
	No	*Low*	*Moderate*	*High*
Risk	_____	_____	_____	
Growth		_____	_____	_____
Income		_____	_____	_____
Tax avoidance	_____		_____	_____

You now have the beginnings of a short-term investment plan—specific goals and an investment strategy (in general terms) for achieving them. To extend your plan, consider the next life event on "Your Life Continuum" and repeat the exercises above, viewing change from your anticipated first life event to the *second life event* as your second transition. When you have recorded final investment factor importance and choice of level rankings for the second transition, compare these to the first for a derivative view of the change that will have to occur in your investment strategy in order to move from successful completion of the first transition to a successful completion of the second. Record this change in Table 2-2.

This derivative view of change would be expanded to include any subsequent additional strategy changes from transition 2 to transition 3, etc., until your plan extends to an appropriate end point. Completion of this analysis provides an extended long-term investment plan when it also includes financial goals discussed earlier. See the end of Chapter 3 for a formal summary of your plan.

Table 2-2. Investment Strategy Change from Transition 1 to Transition 2

	Change in Investment Factor Importance Rankings	
	Transition 1 rank	Transition 2 rank
Risk	_____	_____
Growth	_____	_____
Income	_____	_____
Tax avoidance	_____	_____

	Change in Choice of Level Rankings					
	Transition 1 rank			Transition 2 rank		
Risk	None ___	Low ___	Mod. ___	None ___	Low ___	Mod. ___
Growth	High ___	Mod. ___	Low ___	High ___	Mod. ___	Low ___
Income	High ___	Mod. ___	Low ___	High ___	Mod. ___	Low ___
Tax avoidance	None ___	Mod. ___	High ___	None ___	Mod. ___	High ___

What Does It All Mean? The Story of M.

M was born in 1938. Although his family had been quite wealthy, virtually everything that they had was lost in the 1929 stock market crash. His parents had married in 1930 but were financially unable to establish their own household until a year before M's birth. M's father had found a job with the post office, and the family was barely able to make ends meet during most of M's childhood and adolescence. M was bright, attended a free public university, and graduated with a degree in engineering. After completing his military services obligation, M found employment with a defense contractor, married, and began raising children. At age 52 his two daughters have finished college, M has achieved some occupational success and is now an officer in an airplane manufacturing company.

M wants to invest in mutual funds. When he read the stages of life section of this chapter, he found that his remaining life expectancy was about 25 years, and he developed the following life continuum diagram:

M's Life Continuum

Time: Present	Plus 1 year	Plus 6 years	Plus 13 years	Plus 15 years	Plus 25 years
Critical events: Age 52			Travel	Estate accumulation	
	First daughter's wedding	Second daughter's wedding	Retirement	Move to life-care community	Death: Age 77

M anticipates several important life events associated with his financial goals. He wants to pay for his daughters' weddings, retire comfortably at age 65, spend two years traveling, and then move to a life-care community. Because his childhood was so poverty stricken, he strongly believes in leaving behind a substantial inheritance for his children and possibly grandchildren.

The first part of M's investment plan summary is presented in Table 2-3. With a current net worth of $75,000 and net income of $10,000, M has $25,000 in net cash available for investment. Because of his concerns about leaving an estate, M's quadrant analysis of investment prerequisites revealed that he does not

Table 2-3. M's Investment Plan Summary: Current Status

Net cash available: $25,000

Net income: $10,000

Net worth: $75,000

<table>
<tr><td colspan="3" align="center">Investment Prerequisites Not Adequately Satisfied</td></tr>
<tr><td colspan="3">1. Life insurance</td></tr>
<tr><td colspan="3">2. Access to tax advice</td></tr>
<tr><td colspan="3">3. _____</td></tr>
<tr><td colspan="3">4. _____</td></tr>
<tr><td colspan="3" align="center">Preferences Derived from Trade-Off Analysis</td></tr>
</table>

Importance rank of investment features (risk, growth, income, tax avoidance):

1. Risk
2. Tax avoidance
3. Growth
4. Income

Choice of Levels for Each Investment Factor (1st, 2d, 3d)		
Risk	None: 1st	Low: 2d	Moderate: 3d
Growth	High: 3d	Moderate: 1st	Low: 2d
Income	High: 3d	Moderate: 2d	Low: 1st
Tax avoidance	None: 3d	Moderate: 1st	High: 2d

believe his life insurance program is adequate, although he regards life insurance as highly important. In addition, M recognizes that a large proportion of his salary is withheld in taxes and not recovered as a refund.

So, he would like to have some good advice on how to reduce his tax obligations. The trade-off analysis of M's investment preferences is consistent with his personal background, present concerns, and future expectations. Avoiding risk is most critical among his preferences, followed by moderate tax avoidance and growth. Income is the least among M's current investment preferences, and he would cheerfully trade off income in favor of his other implicit choices.

Next, let's look at the second part of M's investment planning summary, his future plans, represented in Table 2-4. M's financial goals are quite ambitious. Within the next 6 years he hopes

Table 2-4. Financial Goals and Associated Life Events

Financial goal	Associated life event	Anticipated year of occurrence
$25,000 (to spend)	First daughter's wedding	1 year from now
$30,000 (to spend)	Second daughter's wedding	6 years from now
$100,000 (to invest for income)	Retirement	13 years from now
$50,000 (to spend)	Postretirement travel	13 to 15 years from now
$100,000 (to spend)	Entry fee for life-care community	15 years from now
$250,000 (estate)	Bequests to survivors	25 years from now

Investment feature requirements derived from analysis of change (importance rank of investment features—risk, growth, income, tax avoidance)

Transition 1	Transition 2	Transition 3	Transition 4	Transition 5
1. Growth	1. Growth	1. Risk	1. _____	1. _____
2. Risk	2. Risk	2. Income	2. _____	2. _____
3. Tax avoidance	3. Tax avoidance	4. Growth	3. _____	3. _____
4. Income	4. Income	4. Tax avoidance	4. _____	4. _____

Final choice of levels for each investment factor

	Transition 1	Transition 2	Transition 3	Transition 4	Transition 5
Risk (none, low, moderate):	Moderate	Low	Low	_____	_____
Growth (high, moderate, low):	Moderate	Moderate	Low	_____	_____
Income (high, moderate, low):	Low	Low	Moderate	_____	_____
Tax avoidance (none, moderate, high):	Moderate	Moderate	None	_____	_____

Derivative Analysis of Changes in Investment Strategy

Investment strategy changes:
   Between first and second transitions (in words): As retirement approaches, reduce risks.
   Between second and third transitions (in words):
   1. Risk becomes most important and should be kept low.
   2. Income is second in importance and has to be increased to moderate.
   3. Growth becomes third in importance and may be low.
   4. Tax avoidance is least important as retirement income is lower than before and may therefore be low during this period.

to spend $55,000 on his daughters' weddings. Within 13 years he needs to accumulate $100,000 to invest for supplementary retirement income and an additional $50,000 to spend on travel. To enter a life-care community at age 67 he will have to pay an entrance fee of $100,000 in 15 years. Finally, he plans to bequeath $250,000 in legacies upon his death. He will either have to accumulate $150,000 in addition to his $100,000 investment principal or have permanent life insurance for that amount.

Are these goals attainable? The answer is yes: These can be achieved through a consistent and realistic program of savings and investments. Assuming a 10 percent return compounded annually, about what the stock market has averaged in the past, M's $25,000 would grow to $104,431 after 15 years, more than meeting the full cost of entry into a life-care community. If M saves $10,000 per year and reinvests the assumed 10 percent return, in 6 years he will have more then $77,000. M may then spend $30,000 for his second daughter's wedding, invest the remaining $47,000, and continue to add $10,000 in savings annually while reinvesting the presumed 10 percent return. By the time M retires in 13 years he will have $187,000, of which he will spend $50,000 on travel. Assuming no further savings on M's part, he could use the return on $100,000 at 10 percent to supplement his income ($10,000 per year). He still has about $37,000 left over to continue investing for growth, plus the $4000 excess above. By the time he dies this nest egg will have reached about $127,000, which may be added to his $100,000 income-producing investment, for a total of $227,000. M's net worth is currently $75,000, but that includes his original $25,000 stake and an additional $25,000 he will need to liquidate in order to pay for his first daughter's wedding next year. With the remaining $25,000, even if it does not appreciate at all, M's final estate exclusive of life insurance will exceed $250,000 at age 77. How did M figure it out? His computations, using pencil, paper, and a hand calculator are shown in Table 2-5.

M readily identifies his present situation as a hybrid of Moderately Well-off Family-Couple, and he sees three important transitions remaining in his life. The first of these will occur when his 2nd daughter marries. With his planned expenditure of $30,000 for her wedding, M believes he will have fulfilled completely any

Table 2-5. M's Calculations

$25,000 at 10% compounded annually:

End of 1st year:	$ 27,500	
End of 2nd year:	30,250	
End of 3rd year:	33,275	
End of 4th year:	36,603	
End of 5th year:	40,263	
End of 6th year:	44,287	
End of 7th year:	48,718	
End of 8th year:	53,590	
End of 9th year:	58,949	
End of 10th year:	64,844	
End of 11th year:	71,328	
End of 12th year:	78,461	
End of 13th year:	86,307	
End of 14th year:	94,937	
End of 15th year:	104,431 – $100,000 entry fee to life-care community = $4431	

Saving $10,000 per year invested at 10% compounded annually:

End of 1st year:	$ 10,000
End of 2nd year:	11,000 + $10,000 = $21,000
End of 3rd year:	23,100 + $10,000 = $33,100
End of 4th year:	36,410 + $10,000 = $46,410
End of 5th year:	51,051 + $10,000 = $61,051
End of 6th year:	67,156 + $10,000 = $77,156
	– $30,000 for daughter's wedding = $47,156
End of 7th year:	51,872 + $10,000 = $61,872
End of 8th year:	68,059 + $10,000 = $78,059
End of 9th year:	85,865 + $10,000 = $95,865
End of 10th year:	105,452 + $10,000 = $115,452
End of 11th year:	126,997 + $10,000 = $136,997
End of 12th year:	150,697 + $10,000 = $160,697
End of 13th year:	176,767 + $10,000 = $186,767
	– $100,000 for income investments – $50,000 for travel = $36,767
End of 14th year:	40,443
End of 15th year:	44,488 + $4431 excess from life-care fund = $48,919
End of 16th year:	53,811
End of 17th year:	59,192
End of 18th year:	65,111
End of 19th year:	71,622
End of 20th year:	78,785
End of 21st year:	86,663
End of 22nd year:	95,329
End of 23rd year:	104,862
End of 24th year:	115,348
End of 25th year:	126,883

financial commitments he has had to his children during his life-time. After the wedding M and Mrs. M will regard themselves as a moderately well-off couple, at least in financial terms. Taking an objective view of the investment aspects of this transition, M realizes that growth is most important to his investment plans, followed by tax avoidance, risk, and income. Although this ranking exchanges the positions of risk and growth (first and third) in the preference ranking obtained through trade-off analysis, M decides to take his own advice with some modification. He ranks growth first, risk second, tax avoidance third, and income last. His only compromise with preference for choice of levels is in choosing moderate risk; he would prefer none. He also wants moderate growth, moderate tax avoidance, and low income. These choices define M's investment strategy for the next 6 years.

The next transition, from a moderately well-off couple to a "senior" couple traveling for two years and then settling into a life-care community, will occur during the subsequent 9-year period. M does not see any likely change in investment strategy during this period because his needs and preferences will be exactly the same as during the preceding first transition, but risk reduction is called for as he approaches retirement. However, after retirement, when M is in his third and final transitional state, from living to nonliving, M's financial needs will change markedly. Risk is much more important, since M needs income from his investments to pay for his daily expenses and cannot afford to lose every cent of his nest egg. For this reason income must also be ranked more highly. Although the choices M makes for his projected future investment strategy may change in the years ahead, he now has a good idea of where he is going and a strategy for getting there. His next task is to choose a mutual fund investment portfolio that matches his strategy.

What You Should Do Next

Work through the exercises and complete the blank forms and questionnaires supplied. Write your own "Story of M" as a narrative description of your own investment plans using the following worksheet:

Investment Plan Summary: Current Status

Net cash available: _____

Net income: _____

Net worth: _____

Investment Prerequisites Not Adequately Satisfied

1. _____
2. _____
3. _____
4. _____

Preferences Derived from Trade-Off Analysis

1. _____
2. _____
3. _____
4. _____

Choice of Levels for Each Investment Factor (First, Second, Third)

Risk	None _____	Low _____	Moderate _____
Growth	High _____	Moderate _____	Low _____
Income	High _____	Moderate _____	Low _____
Tax avoidance	None _____	Moderate _____	High _____

Financial Goals and Associated Life Events

	Financial goal	*Associated life event*	*Anticipated year of occurrence*
1.	_____	_____	_____
2.	_____	_____	_____
3.	_____	_____	_____
4.	_____	_____	_____
5.	_____	_____	_____

(Continued)

Investment Feature Requirements Derived from Analysis of Change

	Transition 1	Transition 2	Transition 3	Transition 4	Transition 5
1.	_____	_____	_____	_____	_____
2.	_____	_____	_____	_____	_____
3.	_____	_____	_____	_____	_____
4.	_____	_____	_____	_____	_____

First Choice of Levels for Each Investment Factor

	Transition 1	Transition 2	Transition 3	Transition 4	Transition 5
Risk (none, low, moderate):	_____	_____	_____	_____	_____
Growth (high, moderate, low):	_____	_____	_____	_____	_____
Income (high, moderate, low):	_____	_____	_____	_____	_____
Tax avoidance (none, moderate, high):	_____	_____	_____	_____	_____

Derivations Analysis of Changes in Investment Strategy

Investment strategy changes:

   Between first and second transitions (in words):

   Between second and third transitions (in words):

   Between third and fourth transitions (in words):

   Between fourth and fifth transitions (in words):

PART 2

Mutual Fund Basics

In Part 2 you will develop a fundamental understanding of mutual funds. You will learn how a fund operates and how an investor goes about investing in a mutual fund. In addition, Part 2 describes a wide range of funds. The basic background you'll need as an investor is included in this part as well. More detailed elaboration about prospectuses, fees, and related matters are included in Part 4.

3

A Steady Approach

In this chapter you will learn the advantage of a steady investment plan and will consider some examples of get-rich-quick schemes that failed. You will also learn about dollar cost averaging, compound interest, and returns on some other types of investments.

Why a Steady Investment Program Beats Get-Rich-Quick Schemes

A sure, steady, "tortoise" approach to investing is likely to be superior for most people to the quick hit "hare" method, just as winning a big prize in the lottery is not likely to be an effective road to prosperity, though a small number of people have gained riches this way. The odds of a big hit in the stock market are against the investor; just one disastrously bad investment can wipe out a lot of gains from previous good choices. Instead, a carefully thought out long-range plan can do the job. Just as in the fable, slow but steady is the way to go in investing your money.

To illustrate how a slow-but-steady approach can yield outstanding results over time, consider the following three hypothetical investments:

1. An initial investment of $1000 left to accumulate over time at various rates of interest (Table 3-1).

2. An investment that either makes a big profit or a big loss (Table 3-2).

3. A regular investment of $1000 per year (illustrated over various numbers of years) and accumulated at several illustrative interest rates (Table 3-3).

Table 3-1. $1000 Accumulates at Interest

Number of years	5% interest	10% interest	15% interest
0	$ 1,000	$ 1,000	$ 1,000
1	1,050	1,100	1,150
10	1,629	2,594	4,046
20	2,653	6,727	16,367
30	4,322	17,449	66,212
40	7,040	45,259	267,864
50	11,467	117,391	1,083,657
60	18,679	304,482	4,383,999

Table 3-1 assumes that you have $1000 to invest and calculates the total amount you would have after various periods for three rates of interest. Over a few years' time the differences are not great, but over a few decades the amounts earned at different interest rates become quite different.

Table 3-2. Simulation of Total Value Using a Double-or-Nothing Investment Strategy

	Odds of winning (per year)			
Number of years	1 in 2	1 in 5	1 in 10	1 in 20
Starting value	$ 1,000	$ 1,000	$1,000	$1,000
Value after 1 year	2,000	2,000	2,000	2,000
Value after 10 years	1,024,000	1,024,000	0	0
Value after 20 years	0	0	0	0
Value after 30 years	0	0	0	0
Value after 40 years	0	0	0	0
Value after 50 years	0	0	0	0
Value after 60 years	0	0	0	0

As you can see, after 20 years you would almost certainly lose everything, because of the high risks involved.

Table 3-3. A $1000 Investment Per Year at Several
Interest Rates

Number of years	5% interest	10% interest	15% interest	20% interest
0	$ 1,000	$ 1,000	$ 1,000	$ 1,000
1	2,050	2,100	2,150	2,200
10	14,207	18,531	24,349	32,150
20	35,719	64,002	118,810	225,026
30	70,761	181,943	500,957	1,419,258
40	127,840	487,852	2,046,954	8,813,629
50	220,815	1,281,299	8,301,374	54,597,629
60	372,263	3,339,298	33,603,990	338,080,086

By comparison, an investment that each year yields either a 100 percent return or a total loss of your investment produced the results shown in Table 3-2 in a simulated series of trials (about the same as tossing a coin and recording the results, but they vary for each column of the table—they are not all 50-50).

The result of investing $1000 per year and accumulating the earnings over a period of years is illustrated in Table 3-3.

The results of the examples in Tables 3-1 and 3-3 demonstrate that even small amounts invested regularly can produce a sizable total over a few years. The steady approach is likely to yield rich rewards over the years if done carefully. By contrast, the high-risk investor may be lucky for a time and have some big gains, but over time (like the gambler at an Atlantic City casino) the advantage is with the casino or the market.

Big Booms and Big Busts

Some investments can in rare cases bring big gains quickly—but in most cases will bring losses. Commodities futures trading is an example of such an investment. Drilling for oil is another. Over 90 percent of commodities futures trades are said to fail to pay off, yet a small number of commodities trades can produce large profits very quickly. This type of boom-and-bust investing is not recommended to those who use this book. It should only be tried by those with a great deal of investing experience and large amounts of money that they can afford to lose. Some historical examples of investment schemes that seemed to work for a time, then failed are tulip bulbs, Florida real estate, the South Pacific, and chain letters.

A popular theory of markets that has been supported by numerous academic studies in recent years maintains that markets reflect all the available knowledge at any particular time, and the market price for any particular security quickly adjusts to reflect any new information. This seemingly implies that new information would not drastically move the market, because most of the information available has already been incorporated in the price, and new information will just lead to adjustments in the price. Still, there have been instances that dramatically show how markets can move spectacularly upward in seeming defiance of rational behavior and then drop just as suddenly. In recent years, some investors believe that computerized trading can make markets move in violent and irrational ways. Historical examples show that markets have long been subject to seemingly irrational frenzies, fads, and panics.

A classic investment book called *Extraordinary Popular Delusions and the Madness of Crowds* by Charles Mackay (published in 1841) details some extraordinary examples.

Tulipmania

This story is often told as a warning to investors. In brief, tulips entered Europe from Turkey in the mid-1500s. The tulip became popular with the wealthy citizens and then with the general public. Eventually, the Netherlands became a center for cultivating new varieties of the colorful flower, and a market for trading the bulbs developed. A demand for rare varieties developed and began pushing up the prices of the tulip bulbs. By 1625, an especially prized tulip bulb was trading for 2000 guilders, an amount estimated to be equivalent to about $18,000 in today's money. By the time the craze reached its peak in 1637, the 2000-guilder bulb had increased in value by more than 2.5 times its 1625 value to about $50,000. For comparison, Rembrandt was commissioned in 1638 to paint a picture for 1200 guilders. During this speculative binge, prices for ordinary tulip bulbs also escalated. Some people actually sold their possessions and bought tulip bulbs with the money, convinced that they would make a fortune very quickly. In February of 1637, the tulipmania speculation suddenly crashed.

Prices collapsed overnight, and bulbs dropped to 5 percent or less of their precrash levels. Some people who had sold just before the panic set in made large profits, but many others who had waited a bit too long saw their investment drop drastically in value.

The Florida Land Boom of the 1920s

Another example of frenzied trading and speculation pushing prices to absurd levels is the Florida land boom of the 1920s. With the end of World War I and the beginning of a period of optimism and prosperity, Americans were enjoying more leisure time and new freedom to travel. Many Americans acquired automobiles, and an expanded network of passenger trains opened new freedom to travel around the country. Developers realized that the coastal land of southern Florida's east coast could become a gold mine. The region from Palm Beach to Miami saw the most intense speculation. Beach-front property was purchased by developers, who made slight improvements and marketed the land in small lots to northerners looking for vacation or retirement property or speculating for a quick profit. Many investors thought land prices could only go up—there is after all only a limited supply of land. Developers offered property at easy credit terms. The money poured in. Some people put their life savings in Florida land. Many purchasers bought without seeing what they were buying. Some of the land was swamp or otherwise nearly worthless. But investment gurus and celebrities touted the value of Florida land, which further fueled the speculation.

By the spring of 1926, the speculation began to cool. As a shortage of buyers began to develop, prices began to sag. But the frenzy came to an abrupt end in September of 1926, when the worst hurricane in 15 years hit the Florida coast, taking a heavy toll of dead and leaving thousands homeless. By 1927 the land speculation had collapsed, prices had dropped to their prefrenzy level, and many of the real estate agencies had closed.

The South Sea Company

In the early 1700s, England had a huge burden of debt from a war with France and Spain. The Earl of Oxford, among others, offered a plan to have the South Sea Company take over three-fifths of the debt in exchange for a grant of exclusive trading rights to

Central and South America for a payment to the government of 7 million pounds. After assuming the debt, the South Sea Company issued stock. In 1720, London was swept up in a wave of frenzied speculation as people bid up the price of South Sea Company stock even though the company had still not done any trading with Central and South America. In March of 1720, a share of the stock was selling for about 130 pounds. By May, the price had climbed to 890 pounds. Seemingly everyone wanted to own South Sea Company's stock. The king and many members of parliament were stockholders. The excitement inspired other ambitious entrepreneurs to sell stock to launch new ventures. Many were ill-advised and quickly failed. One entrepreneur even offered new shares in a venture so secret the stockholders could not be told its purpose. After collecting the proceeds, he disappeared.

By the summer of 1720, investors were growing nervous about the high price of South Sea shares. When the price dropped a few percentage points, the company tried to prop up the price by lending investors money to buy more stock and paying (and promising) large dividends. But the effort failed, and the stock price collapsed. Among the investors who lost heavily was Sir Isaac Newton who, despite explaining how the planets move through the solar system, apparently had not mastered the psychology of markets. He lost 20,000 pounds.

Chain Letters

In addition to investment manias, there are frauds which exploit the same psychology. For example, most people have received chain letters from time to time. These letters promise high returns if you simply send a small amount of money to a person earlier on the list and send the letter to a few more people. The logic is simple but flawed. If everyone sends money to the people above them on the list and sends the letter to several more people, logically the letter will soon be going to many people who will be sending money to previous letter senders and soon everyone will be rich. Unfortunately, even if everyone who received the letter acted on it, the numbers of people who would have to be involved would soon become astronomically large, so the chain quickly breaks down.

A related and time-honored fraud that continues to be perpetrated on investors to this day is called the Ponzi scheme. Just as in the chain letter, the earliest people involved get paid by later "investors" until, inevitably, the scheme runs short of new entrants and falls apart.

The Logic of Long-term Investing

Most investors will profit from a relatively long-term approach that involves putting an initial sum in a carefully considered investment or portfolio of investments and adding some additional sums at regular intervals if possible. At appropriate intervals the logic of the portfolio should also be reconsidered and revised if necessary.

Dollar Cost Averaging

Dollar cost averaging is an important element in a long-term investment strategy. Dollar cost averaging simply means to invest at regular intervals. If each new investment is for a fixed amount, for example $1000 a year or $100 a month, then if the market drops, your next investment will buy a larger number of shares. As the market goes up you will get fewer shares with your new purchase, but your existing shares will be worth more. Over time, this will maximize your investment effectiveness without requiring you to determine the "best time" to buy. If you use dollar cost averaging, the best time is now and next month and the month after that.

The Power of Compound Interest

The power of compound interest can be startling. Many savers have been annoyed by the disturbingly slow appreciation of their money in a savings account. They may have difficulty recognizing it, but compound interest (interest where the interest payments are left to accumulate and earn additional interest) has amazing power to generate large amounts from relatively small initial deposits. To work well, however, the money should be left to accumulate over a reasonably long period of time free from withdrawals and taxes.

According to a well-known story, the Dutchman Peter Minuit

bought the island of Manhattan from the natives in the fall of the year 1626 for about $24 worth of trinkets. Consider what would have happened if Peter Minuit had invested the $24 at compound interest from 1626 to 1990, a period of 364 years. Assuming that no taxes had to be paid out of the proceeds and that the interest rate was 6 percent over the entire time, the $24 would have grown to $39,043,271,259 by the fall of 1990.

The interest rate is a crucial factor in compound interest rate performance. If Peter Minuit's money could have earned 10 percent per year, it would have grown to $27,999,394,479,600,000 over the same period. This is far more than the current value of all land, buildings, stocks, bonds, and other assets in the entire world.

The other crucial factor in allowing compound interest to work its inexorable magic is time. The power of compounding is not so clear over a few months or a few years but becomes strikingly obvious over decades or longer periods.

Benjamin Franklin, that versatile U.S. genius, recognized the power of compound interest in a pair of bequests he made in his will to the cities of Boston and Philadelphia. Each was given 1000 pounds upon Franklin's death in 1790 with instructions about how the money was to be used over the next 100 years. In 1890 part of the money was disbursed. Franklin specified that the remaining money should be divided among the cities of Boston and Philadelphia and states of Massachusetts and Pennsylvania after 200 years had elapsed following his death. Franklin's will stated that he did not presume to carry his views further than 200 years. Although some of the money from each city was lent at interest or spent for various purposes that came under the terms of Franklin's will, by early 1990, the time Franklin had specified for the end of the experiment, the Boston fund had $4.5 million left from the bequest and Philadelphia had $2 million remaining. Incidentally, the 2000 pounds came from the salary he earned as governor of Pennsylvania from 1785 to 1788 and was in keeping with his idea that public servants in a democracy should not be paid.

If you accept the notion that the power of compound interest to increase your investment money is impressive, you might still object that real investments do not often meet the requirements that there be no taxes payable and the investment yield a steady return over many years. But there are ways to approximate these requirements using IRAs, or 401(k)s, or such investments as zero-coupon (or other) municipal bonds.

Zero-Coupon Bonds and Compound Interest

Long-term zero-coupon bonds also demonstrate the efficiency of compound interest. For a small investment, a "zero" can accumulate to a large amount. Zero-coupon bonds are bonds that are sold at a discount from their face amount and pay no interest, rather like the government savings bonds you may buy through payroll deduction at work. Since they pay no interest, the discount can be quite substantial. For example, on August 6, 1990, the *Wall Street Journal* quoted one representative zero-coupon bond due in the year 2000 at $39 per $100 of face amount and another due in 2004 at $40.50, whereas a government Treasury "strip" which will be worth $100 in May of 2020 was selling for about $9.00.

Assume that you would like to become a millionaire. How much would you have to invest to become a millionaire in a certain period? If the investment is assumed to be tax-free, Table 3-4 shows how much you need to invest initially at various interest rates to have $1 million at the end of various periods. So if you could be assured of getting 15 percent interest over 40 years, you

Table 3-4. Investing to Accumulate $1 Million

	Interest		
Years	5%	10%	15%
1	952,381	909,091	869,565
5	783,526	620,921	497,177
10	613,913	385,543	247,185
15	481,017	239,392	122,894
20	376,889	148,644	61,100
25	295,303	92,296	30,378
30	231,377	57,086	15,103
35	181,290	35,584	7,509
40	142,046	22,095	3,733

could become a millionaire by investing only $3733 because of the power of compound interest (assuming you did not have to pay taxes on the earnings).

Numerous academic and business studies have shown that over a long enough period, common stocks have led all types of investments in return. For example, an analysis discussed in *The New York Times* in June 1990,[1] stated that $1 invested in 1926, in common stocks as measured by the Standard and Poor's 500 stock index would have grown to $535 by 1989, a 10½ percent compound annual growth rate. Similarly, a $1 investment in intermediate-term Treasury bonds would be worth $22, a 5 percent compound annual growth rate. Treasury bills would have grown a $1 investment to $10, a 3.7 percent annual growth rate. Stocks would have shown positive returns in 45 years and losses in 19 years; Treasury bonds showed gains in 58 years and losses in 6 years; Treasury bills showed positive returns in all 64 years.

Real Estate

Real estate has generally been a profitable investment for Americans. Many who purchased homes in recent decades have had the pleasant experience of seeing the value of their dwelling grow greatly in price while they used it for its main purpose—as a place to live and raise a family. Furthermore, it has been said that 90 percent of U.S. millionaires made their money in real estate. Many started with a small amount of money and bought properties with a big mortgage and a lot of leverage. Still, investing in real estate is often difficult and risky and requires substantial in-depth knowledge about the particular types of properties and the specific markets in which they are located. The experiences of the 1980s in many parts of the Southwest and Midwest demonstrated that it is quite possible to lose a lot of money in real estate.

There are some other obstacles as well. Unless the investor has substantial resources, a small number of investments may deplete all the investor's investable funds—precluding the type of diversification that would normally be desirable. Also, real estate transactions can involve large transaction and maintenance charges

---

[1]Jan M. Rosen, "Your Money," *The New York Times,* June 30, 1990, p. 32.

that unless carefully analyzed can have a major impact on the profitability of the investments. Real estate is a rather illiquid investment. It can be difficult to sell a property when you decide to get out. A difficult real estate market, a tenant who refuses to vacate the property, or other unanticipated circumstances can complicate an attempt to sell. Local regulations and conditions such as rent controls and court rulings about tenants' rights can also affect profitability. Most people are not equipped to adequately evaluate all these considerations and to provide the type of professional management that may be required. It is possible to participate in pooled ownership of real estate through REITs (real estate investment trusts) which are similar in some ways to mutual funds. But the differences from mutual funds are substantial enough that a full discussion of REITs is beyond the scope of this book.

Antiques

Many people who enjoy the decorative quality of antiques understandably consider the possibility that they may be attractive investments as well. Although it is possible to make money investing in antiques, it is not easy. Knowing what antiques will appreciate in value is part of the problem. Some violins made in Cremona, Italy, grew old and valuable since the seventeenth and eighteenth centuries; others just grew old. How can you tell what items will become valuable over the years? It is probably more art and intuition than science. Assuming you could recognize which antiques to buy, you could make a profit if you could buy at a good price and sell without paying too much in transaction fees. But antiques are not very liquid investments, and selling at a good price may be difficult when you decide to dispose of the investment. Until you sell your antiques, they produce no income and may require substantial payments in the form of security devices and insurance premiums.

Art

The art world is rocked from time to time by the news of a spectacular auction of a famous painting (or other work) for a price that sets new records. This causes art critics to decry the commercialization of art and long for the days before prices were driven sky high by such frenzied buying. A casual observer might conclude that art is the ideal investment—guaranteed to sell for more in the future and fun to look at until you decide to sell. But art is not a sure investment, except for a small number of well-known masterpieces by a few great and already famous artists such as Van Gogh or Picasso. Paintings of this type seldom come on the market. When they do, they are already selling for such high prices that they are not practical investments for most investors.

Art by current, little-known artists who may eventually become famous could be an entree to the market by the small investor. But spotting artists of great promise before they become famous is something that few investors may be equipped to do, and the payoff may not come for decades. During the time until the artist becomes famous, the art is not paying dividends and may be difficult to sell if you decide to cash in your portfolio.

Even buying a little-recognized masterpiece by a great but still unknown artist is not as profitable as the headlines may imply. A record-setting sale of a Van Gogh painting in 1987 brought in a reported $39.9 million. The same painting had been sold a few months after Vincent Van Gogh's death in 1890 for approximately $100. So the return was a compound annual rate of 14 percent. Although this is not a bad return, there are mutual funds which have had a higher return over several decades.

Conclusion

Unless you are a bona fide expert with special insight into the values associated with the investment aspects of securities, real estate, antiques, or art, you will be better off investing your money in mutual funds than in these areas. Mutual fund management experts provide specialized knowledge on a full-time basis and are professionally competent where you may not be.

4

Investing in Mutual Funds

In this chapter you will learn about the possibilities for investing and about a brief history of mutual funds. In addition, we provide answers to common questions about mutual funds and a review of common types of funds and their performance.

The Investor's Dilemma—
What to Invest In?

Once you make the decision to invest, one of the first, most important, and most baffling questions to be faced is "What should I invest in?" There are many potential investment vehicles to choose from—including real estate, securities, race horses, stamps, gold, commodity futures, rare books, art, coins, and others. The following list shows some of the possibilities:

Stocks	Corporate bonds
Residential real estate	Bank CDs
Race horses	Art
Commercial real estate	Options
Stamps	Coins
Rare books	Ginnie Maes
Mutual funds	Overseas investments
Commodity futures	Treasury securities

Penny stocks	Municipal bonds
Initial offerings of stocks	Annuities
Antiques	Gold

A little investigating will probably convince you that many of these options are too risky or otherwise impractical for the majority of investors. So like most investors, you will probably conclude that the realistic number of choices is considerably smaller. Experience revealed in many studies has shown that financial assets, specifically common stocks, have been the investment with the best long-term investment return. The prime choice for most investors should be common stocks, but there are a number of difficulties for the average investor who wants to invest in common stock. One problem is that common stocks, although high yielding over a long period, can be very volatile over shorter intervals. Even casual newspaper readers or television news watchers will be aware that the stock market sometimes drops drastically and unexpectedly. One financial advisor suggests that investors should be prepared to withstand a 30 percent paper loss in any year. If you have invested heavily in the stock market and a downturn such as the October 1987 crash takes place, you may have to be prepared to wait for an indefinite time before withdrawing your invested money or be prepared to take a significant loss. So your investment capital may be tied up for a long time. Thus you should not put money in the stock market that you may need to withdraw within the next couple of years.

Picking stocks is another problem. Picking stocks and watching them gain or lose value can be an interesting pastime, but few investors have the time, skill, or patience to gain the knowledge and experience that are required to confidently select appropriate stocks and to decide when to buy or sell. Professional money managers often work long hours and use complex techniques as well as in-depth knowledge of the companies, the managers, and the markets in their pursuit of profitable stocks. Most individual investors do not have the time, skill, access to corporate managements, or interest that would be required to match their efforts.

Transaction costs pose another major hurdle. The cost of buying and selling stocks, even if you search out the lowest commissions at discount brokerage firms, means that the stock may have to increase in value substantially just to break even. Indeed, after paying your broker's commissions and subtracting the taxes payable on your gain, you may find that what seemed to be a nice gain largely evaporates. The loss of buying power of your money, because of inflation during the time you held your investment, may further deflate your seemingly attractive gain.

Most investors do not have enough money to seek the money management services of a professional. Being a small investor in today's volatile markets can seem almost as though you are trapped in a stampede of elephants as the institutional traders buy or sell huge amounts of stock.

Small investors generally do not have enough money to diversify their investment portfolio adequately. One hundred shares of a stock selling for $50 each will cost the investor $5000, not including commissions. Assuming that the investor wants 20 different stocks in his or her portfolio to ensure adequate diversification, it would be necessary to invest about $100,000. Lower-priced stocks would require a little less money, but clearly many investors would not be able to invest enough money to gain adequate diversification.

So what should you do? It is beginning to seem as though there may be no solution to the small investor's plight. Fortunately, that is not the case. *Mutual funds are the answer.*

A Brief History of Mutual Funds

The first U.S. mutual fund was formed in Boston in 1924. It was based on an idea that originated in Europe in the nineteenth century.

In 1936, following the 1929 crash and during the bleak days of the Depression, the Securities and Exchange Commission (SEC) was mandated by Congress to investigate investment companies. The study led to the Investment Company Act of 1940, the basic law regulating mutual funds.

In 1940, when the basic legislation was passed, there were 68 mutual funds with $448 million in assets and 296,000 shareholder accounts. A few of these funds invested in bonds in 1940, but by and large they were a way of investing in stocks. The proliferation of types of funds did not take place until many years later. The mutual fund industry attained $1 billion of assets in 1945 and 1 million accounts in 1951.

By the early 1970s the industry had grown to almost 400 funds and $50 billion in assets, but the big change in mutual funds came during the time of high interest rates in the 1970s when many small investors moved money from banks and thrifts to money market funds to reap the rewards of high interest rates. Having become acquainted with funds, many began putting money in other types of funds, including some of the vast number of newly created funds that emerged in the rest of the 1970s and throughout the 1980s.

By the end of 1989, mutual funds assets totalled more than $900 billion, and mutual funds were owned by 22.8 million U.S. households. Bond and income funds made up 31 percent of mutual fund assets; equity, 25.4 percent; and money market and short-term municipals, 43.6 percent.

The total assets of stock and bond mutual funds grew little during the 1970s but experienced rapid growth in the 1980s. By the end of the 1970s, money market funds, which had been introduced during the decade, had grown to represent one-half of mutual fund assets. They continued to grow during the 1980s, but the relatively strong economy and the boom in the financial markets during much of the 1980s attracted much new money into stock and bond funds as well. Assets of money market funds grew from $45.2 billion at the end of 1979 to $358.7 billion at the end of 1989; equity, bond, and income funds grew from $49 billion to $553.9 billion; and short-term municipal bond funds grew from $0.3 billion to $69.4 billion. Cumulative growth in mutual fund assets was up 939 percent for the decade.

Mutual fund companies responded to the high bond yields and the influx of money during the 1980s by creating many new types of bond funds with various combinations of risk and reward. Sales of bond funds grew accordingly.

All in all, about 2400 new funds and 18 new types of funds were created during the 1980s; despite the 1987 stock market crash, the industry had impressive growth for the decade.

Questions about Mutual Funds

Why Do Mutual Funds Exist?

Mutual funds exist to give small investors an alternative way to invest in capital markets and to provide an alternative source of money to finance industries by buying their securities.

Mutual funds also allow small investors to have a measure of self-defense when investing in markets which have become increasingly dominated by giant financial institutions. By buying shares in a mutual fund, the individual becomes part of an institution and so can stand on more even terms.

Why Should You Consider Mutual Funds Your Primary Investment Vehicle?

Many investment advisors have urged individual investors to rely on mutual funds in recent years. An example of such a recommendation is the one from asset allocator David Kurdish as reported in *Forbes* magazine (October 1990).[1] *Forbes* reports that Kurdish tells people with "less than $5 million or $10 million" to go into no-load mutual funds. Kurdish believes transaction costs are too high for the small investor who tries to diversify a small portfolio, so it is cheaper to pay a no-load fund's management fee. Kurdish explains: "The firm taking a $5 million account won't pay 6 cents a share in transactions. It'll pay 20 cents. A bank will hold the assets. Between transaction costs, investment management fees, custodial costs, you're talking 3 percent a year to have an active manager. And you have no diversification. You have one equity style, one bond style. Why not have a series of no-load mutual funds." The article concludes, "That's the nice thing about no-load funds. A small investor—and today anything under $5 million is a small portfolio—can use them to create his own asset allocation system and still achieve the same economies of scale a big investor gets."

How Do Mutual Funds Operate?

Mutual funds are organized, operated, and managed by companies that do the practical administrative things that allow the fund to function. They select the fund's strategy, hire the managers, market the shares to potential investors, and do the paper work (keeping records of shareowners' holdings; sending statements, proxies, and other material to the investors; redeeming shares of shareowners who decide to cash out; etc.).

There are almost 300 mutual fund management companies, including some very large ones that operate many funds. One of the

---

[1] Marcia Berss, "The Money Men," *Forbes,* October 1, 1990, pp. 216–220.

largest fund managers, Fidelity, has well over 100 funds listed in the newspaper mutual fund quotations as of September 1990. The 1980s have been years of rapid growth for mutual funds, and many fund managers have added new funds to give their investors a broad range of choices, thereby trying to keep most of or all their investments in the same fund family.

Most no-load funds are purchased directly from the fund's sponsoring company, in contrast to load funds which are frequently purchased through brokers and financial advisors or financial planners who receive a fee for their services.

Another way to purchase no-load funds is to buy them through a discount brokerage firm. At least one major discount broker, Charles Schwab, offers a convenient way to purchase a selected group of no-load funds, about 400 funds as of September 1990. The discount broker charges a fee which partly offsets the main advantage of no-load funds (no fee), but the plan offers certain conveniences such as quickly transferring money out of one fund into a fund in a different family which may justify the extra fee for some investors. This is an especially appealing feature to investors who like to frequently reevaluate their investments and shift money to other funds. But check carefully before investing to determine if the broker's plan includes the funds you might want to invest in and to determine what fees you will be charged.

Why Should You Prefer One Family of Funds over Another?

Some fund families, as a whole or in some of their individual funds, have established outstanding records of performance (growth of net asset value per share) over impressive periods. Some investors buy funds on the strength of such performance ratings, which are published in a number of financial publications. Some of these publications not only give rankings based on how well the fund has performed over some period (the last quarter, year, 5 years, or 10 years) but compile indexes which they claim will help the investor to evaluate the fund's ability to perform in a rising market or a falling market. Any of these lists can provide useful information, but investors should always be aware that the future performance of any fund will probably not be a replay of its past performance. Many factors that will affect the performance of a fund can change (the economy, market psychology, management of the funds, etc.).

What about the Fund Managers?

Some people consider the manager of the fund to be an important consideration in deciding which fund to buy. Although the names of many fund managers are hardly household names and would not be much help to the average investor in evaluating the likely performance of the fund, a few money managers have become almost legendary among knowledgeable investors.

Peter Lynch, who retired in mid-1990 after guiding the Fidelity Magellan Fund to years of outstanding performance, is an example of such a manager. For investors who follow fund managers, some mutual fund listings identify the manager of each listed fund and give the length of time the manager has been in charge of that fund. Although this can be a useful technique, it is not infallible. Having a good record for a while does not guarantee that a manager will have continued success.

What Types of Funds Are Offered by the Family?

A family of funds may have many funds or only a few. Some investors like the flexibility of being able to choose among a broad array of funds and change their choices from time to time as market conditions, or their perception of market conditions, change. For such an investor, the number of funds and the specific types of funds offered by the family may be important.

How Many Types of Funds Are There?

Although there are many types of funds, including slight variations of the basic types, the *Mutual Fund Fact Book,*[2] lists 22 basic types of mutual funds:

1. Aggressive growth funds
2. Balanced funds
3. Corporate bond funds

[2]*Mutual Fund Fact Book: 1990,* Investment Company Institute, Washington, D.C., pp. 17–18.

4. Flexible portfolio funds
5. GNMA or Ginnie Mae funds
6. Global bond funds
7. Global equity funds
8. Growth funds
9. Growth and income funds
10. High-yield bond funds
11. Income (bond) funds
12. Income (equity) funds
13. Income (mixed) funds
14. International funds
15. Long-term municipal bond funds
16. Money market funds
17. Option/income funds
18. Precious metals, gold funds
19. Short-term municipal bond funds
20. State municipal bond funds—long-term
21. State municipal bond funds—short-term
22. U.S. government income funds

Note that some popular types of funds do not appear on this list, for example, selected industry funds. These additional types can be considered as subclassifications of one of the types listed above.

Your Dealings with Mutual Funds

Assume that you have completed the analysis described in this book and have decided to invest in a portfolio of mutual funds. One of the (hypothetical) funds you have selected to be part of your portfolio is called the Widget Industry Select Fund. It invests in stocks of companies that manufacture widgets. You believe that widgets will sell like the proverbial hotcakes during the 1990s, and so you want to invest in a widget fund. You are aware of the reduced degree of diversification you get by investing in an industry fund. Indeed, you want more limited diversification, since you are thoroughly convinced that widgets are the growth industry of the next few years, and you are loath to have your expected fast growth diluted by investments in slower-growth industries as they would be in more diversified funds.

You realize that you are assuming some additional risk by taking this approach, yet you have decided that it is appropriate to take this additional risk. For example, the widget fund owns mostly shares of such companies as American Widget International, National Widget Ltd., and Nippon Widgets. So if the widget industry experiences a downturn, the fund could suffer more than more diversified funds.

The Widget Industry Select Fund is one of a family of funds managed by the Gargantuan Group, a (nonexistent) fund management company that sponsors many types of funds, including many industry select funds. You are impressed by the track record of many of the Gargantuan family's funds, and the widget fund is managed by an impressive young manager whom you read about in a financial publication. So now you are ready to put $2000 of the money from your investment portfolio in this fund. What do you do? You recall that you saw an advertisement for this fund in a newspaper recently. You still have the newspaper in your pile for the recycling bin, so you retrieve it, look up the financial section, and tear out the ad. You discover that you can fill in your name and address and mail the ad to the fund or you can call a telephone number listed on the advertisement. You decide to call the number. After going through one of those annoying automated systems where you punch buttons to indicate what you are interested in ("1 for health food select funds, . . . 2 for the high-risk, low-return fund, . . . 3 for the fund that invests in bankrupt companies, . . . 132 for cashing in your existing fund shares") you finally get to talk to a human representative. You request a prospectus (brochure that describes the essential things you should know about the fund before investing—such as the investment objective and the fees and charges associated with the fund) and some other literature about the fund and its manager.

After a few days you receive a packet of literature from Gargantuan containing an application form, a prospectus for the widget fund, and some information about the Gargantuan organization and its other funds. Finally, having reviewed the prospectus and considered the charge levied by the fund (an annual management fee of 2 percent of the fund's assets) you write a check for $2000 to the Gargantuan Widget Fund, you complete the application forms, and you mail them to Gargantuan's headquarters in Punxsutawney, Pennsylvania.

After a couple of weeks, you receive a confirmation notice in the mail showing that you purchased $2000 worth of the widget fund a few days after you mailed your check (the day they processed your check). The price you paid for each share was the price listed in the newspaper for the day of your transaction. Your no-load shares were worth $2000 immediately after you purchased them. If you had purchased shares in an 8 percent load fund instead, the funds would have had a total value of $1840 immediately following the purchase, $2000 minus your 8 percent "load" charge ($160).

What will the shares be worth the next day, or the day after that? That, of course, depends on the performance of the stocks (mostly widget companies) that the fund owns. If the economy is strong, investors have bullish outlooks, and the demand for widgets grows rapidly, as you had expected, your widget shares may grow rapidly in value. You can track their performance each day by looking in the financial pages of the newspaper for the mutual fund prices. To get the total value of your widget shares, you must multiply the price listed in the newspaper (the per-share price) by the number of shares you own. Part of the fun of investing in mutual funds comes from the sense of anticipation as you open the financial pages each day to see how your funds did yesterday. Of course, it is the long-term results over several months or years rather than the day-to-day fluctuations that really matter.

With skillful selection and a bit of good luck, a couple of years have gone by since you made your widget investment and you now have a nice profit on paper, but you are less optimistic about widgets than you had previously been. You believe that the widget craze may have run its course, and widget demand may be about to fall. Furthermore, in reviewing your asset allocation, you decide that it is time to reduce a little of the risk in your portfolio and increase diversity. You decide it is time to sell your holdings of the Gargantuan family Widget Industry Select Fund. So how do you proceed?

You call Punxsutawney and tell a representative to cash in your holdings and send a check. A few days or weeks later you receive a check for the current value of your widget shares and a statement telling you the number of shares you sold and the selling price. Note that for large amounts (typically $10,000 or more) you may have to send your request in writing with a signature that has been "guaranteed" by a third party. Check the prospectus or call the fund for their particular rules.

Some bond and money market funds offer the alternative of writing a check against the balance in your account to allow quicker access to your money when you decide to cash in your shares. Some other possible ways of redeeming money in your mutual fund shares would be to write to the fund manager and ask to have your money sent to you. You want to have the money from your widget fund transferred to another fund in the Gargantuan family; you may be able to call Gargantuan and give them instructions for the switch and have it carried out immediately. The exact redemption methods available will depend on the procedures of your fund family and should be described in the fund material you received along with the prospectus.

Types of Mutual Funds

The following is a list of the major categories.[3]

Aggressive Growth Funds: These funds seek maximum capital gains as their investment objective. Current income is not a significant factor. Some may invest in stocks of businesses that are somewhat out of the mainstream, such as fledgling companies, new industries, companies fallen on hard times, or industries temporarily out of favor. Some may also use specialized investment techniques such as option writing or short-term trading.

Balanced Funds: Generally these funds have a three-part investment objective: (1) to conserve the investors' initial principal, (2) to pay current income, (3) to promote long-term growth of both this principal and income. Balanced funds have a portfolio mix of bonds, preferred stocks, and common stocks.

Corporate Bond Funds: Like income funds, these funds seek a high level of income. They do so by buying bonds of corporations

---

[3]Source: *Mutual Fund Fact Book: 1990,* Investment Company Institute, Washington, D.C. (Reprinted with permission.)

for the majority of the fund's portfolio. The rest of the portfolio may be in U.S. Treasury bonds or bonds issued by a federal agency.

Flexible Portfolio Funds: These funds may be 100 percent invested in stocks or bonds or money market instruments depending on market conditions. These funds give the money managers the greatest flexibility in anticipating or responding to economic changes.

GNMA or Ginnie Mae Funds: These funds invest in mortgage securities backed by the Government National Mortgage Association (GNMA). To qualify for this category, the majority of the portfolio must always be invested in mortgage-backed securities.

Global Bond Funds: These funds invest in the debt securities of companies and countries worldwide, including the United States.

Global Equity Funds: These funds invest in securities traded worldwide, including the United States. Compared to direct investments, global funds offer investors an easier avenue to investing abroad. The funds' professional money managers handle the trading and record keeping details and deal with differences in currencies, languages, time zones, laws and regulations, and business customs and practices. In addition to another layer of diversification, global funds add another layer of risk—exchange-rate risk.

Growth Funds: Growth funds invest in the common stock of well-established companies. Their primary aim is to produce an increase in the value of their investments (capital gains) rather than a flow of dividends. Investors who buy a growth fund are more interested in seeing the fund's share price rise than in receiving income from dividends.

Growth and Income Funds: These funds invest mainly in the common stock of companies that have had increasing share value but also a solid record of paying dividends. This type of fund attempts to combine long-term capital growth with a steady stream of income.

High-Yield Bond Funds: These funds maintain at least two-thirds of their portfolios in lower-rated corporate bonds (Baa or lower by Moody's rating service and BBB or lower by Standard and Poor's rating service). In return for a generally higher yield, investors must bear a greater degree of risk than for higher-rated bonds.

Income (Bond) Funds: Income bond funds seek a high level of current income for their shareholders by investing at all times in a mix of corporate and government bonds.

Income (Equity) Funds: Income equity funds seek a high level of current income for their shareholders by investing primarily in equity securities of companies with good dividend-paying records.

Income (Mixed) Funds: Mixed income funds seek a high level of current income for their shareholders by investing in income-producing securities, including both equities and debt instruments.

International Funds: International funds invest in equity securities of companies located outside the United States. Two-thirds of their portfolios must be so invested at all times to be categorized here.

Long-term Municipal Bond Funds: These funds invest in bonds issued by states and municipalities to finance schools, highways, hospitals, airports, bridges, water and sewer works, and other public projects. In most cases, income earned on these securities is not taxed by the federal government but may be taxed under state and local laws. For some taxpayers, portions of income earned on these securities may be subject to the federal alternative minimum tax.

Money Market Mutual Funds: These funds invest in the short-term securities sold in the money market. These are generally the safest, most stable securities available, including Treasury bills, certificates of deposit of large banks, and commercial paper (the short-term IOUs of large U.S. corporations).

Option/Income Funds: These funds seek a higher current return by investing primarily in dividend-paying common stocks on which call options are traded on national securities exchanges. Current return generally consists of dividends, premiums from writing options, net short-term gains from sales of portfolio securities on exercises of options or otherwise, and any profits from closing purchase transactions.

Precious Metals, Gold Funds: These funds maintain two-thirds of their portfolios invested in securities associated with gold, silver, and other precious metals.

Short-term Municipal Bond Funds: These funds invest in municipal securities with relatively short maturities. These are also known as "tax-exempt money market funds." For some taxpayers, portions of income from these securities may be subject to the federal alternative minimum tax.

State Municipal Bond Funds—Long-term: These funds work just like other long-term municipal bond funds (see page 91) except their portfolios contain the issues of only one state. A resident of that state has the advantage of receiving income free of both federal and state tax. For some taxpayers, portions of income from these securities may be subject to the federal alternative minimum tax.

State Municipal Bond Funds—Short-term: These funds work just like other short-term municipal bond funds (see page 91) except their portfolios contain the issues of only one state. A resident of that state has the advantage of receiving income free of both federal and state tax. For some taxpayers, portions of income from these securities may be subject to the federal alternative minimum tax.

U.S. Government Income Funds: These funds invest in a variety of government securities. These include U.S. Treasury bonds, federally guaranteed mortgage-backed securities, and other government notes.

Some statistics about each of the various types of funds (number of funds, assets, and sales) are shown in Table 4-1.

How Do the Different Types of Funds Perform?

The Handbook for No-Load Fund Investors reports on performance for fund groups (see Table 4-2) over three time periods as compared to several stock market and inflation indices.

Table 4-1. Mutual Funds, Assets, Sales

	Number of funds (1989)	Assets (1989) (billions)	Sales (1989) (billions)
Aggressive growth	213	$37.2	$ 8,577.8
Growth	352	66.1	12,432.6
Growth and income	271	91.4	21,944.4
Precious metals	36	4.1	998.9
International	75	9.9	2,456.7
Global equity	48	13.7	2,224.0
Income equity	73	22.9	5,380.7
Option/income	13	3.8	448.8
Flexible portfolio	45	4.1	1,194.7
Balanced	59	13.5	2,090.8
Income (mix)	75	15.2	7,251.3
Income (bond)	102	13.4	4,457.4
U.S. government income	205	81.4	11,797.1
Ginnie Mae	57	28.2	3,771.0
Global bond	29	3.1	893.9
Corporate bond	58	11.7	3,179.4
High-yield bond	104	28.5	9,866.8
Long-term municipal	180	64.5	15,470.0
State municipal (long-term)	258	41.2	11,277.0
Short-term municipal	129	NA	NA
State municipal (short-term)	72	NA	NA
Money market	4632	NA	NA

Adapted from *Mutual Funds Fact Book: 1990,* Investment Company Institute, Washington, D.C., with permission.

Table 4-2. Performance Summary

No-load fund	1991	Total return 5 years, annualized (1987–1991)	10 years, annualized (1982–1991)
All stock funds	30.8%	11.7%	13.6%
All diversified stock*	33.2	12.0	13.7
Aggressive growth	45.2	12.9	12.0
Growth	32.0	12.3	14.1
Growth income	27.4	11.6	14.7
Income	25.1	10.1	14.5
Asset allocation	21.4	11.9	—
Asset allocation, global	13.9	7.3	—
Balanced	24.7	12.5	16.4
Convertible funds	32.5	9.5	13.5
Financial	59.4	11.5	16.2
Health	79.6	29.8	27.3
Global stock	18.0	13.1	—
International stock	12.2	9.2	15.2
Natural resources	4.5	7.6	10.0
Precious metals	−6.0	−0.3	2.7
Small-company growth	49.1	13.6	13.1
Technology	48.6	13.2	13.3
Utilities	23.5	10.1	16.1
Fixed income—total	15.6	8.5	12.7
Fixed income—corporate, short-term	11.5	7.9	11.6
Fixed income—corporate, intermediate	15.2	8.5	12.3
Fixed income—corporate, long-term	16.7	8.6	13.1
Fixed income—high-yield	30.4	6.1	13.0
Fixed income—government, short-term	11.6	7.7	10.6
Fixed income—government, intermediate	15.0	9.2	13.7
Fixed income—government, long-term	15.4	8.9	12.4

Table 4-2. Performance Summary (*Continued*)

		Total return	
No-load fund	1991	5 years, annualized (1987–1991)	10 years, annualized (1982–1991)
Fixed income—world	11.1%	10.9%	—
Tax-free—total	11.2	7.1	12.3
Tax-free—short-term	8.2	5.8	7.6
Tax-free—intermediate	10.5	7.1	11.5
Tax-free—long-term	11.9	7.6	13.4
Tax-free—high-yield	11.7	7.8	13.5
Tax-free—NY	12.5	6.9	10.1
Tax-free—CA	10.9	6.7	—
Tax-free—MA	12.2	7.1	—
Money market general	5.8	7.1	8.1
Money market government	5.6	6.8	7.8
Money market tax-free	3.6	4.8	5.2
Closed-end bond	20.1	10.5	14.2
Closed-end international	16.4	23.4	—
Stock market indices			
S&P 500 with reinvestment	30.4	15.4	17.5
Dow Jones Industrials†	20.3	10.8	13.8
S&P 500†	26.3	11.5	13.0
NYSE Composite†	27.1	10.6	12.4
American Stock Exchange†	28.2	8.4	9.4
Value Line Composite†	27.2	2.0	6.1
NASDAQ Composite†	56.8	13.3	12.8
Wilshire 5000†	30.3	10.7	12.1
Morgan Stanley EAFE in $US	12.5	9.0	16.1
Morgan Stanley Gold Mines†	−8.1	−0.7	−1.8
Consumer Price Index	3.1	4.5	3.9

*Average of aggressive growth, growth, growth-income, and income funds.
†Without dividends reinvested.
SOURCE: Sheldon Jacobs, *The Handbook for No-Load Fund Investors,* The No-Load Fund Investor, Inc., 1991. (*Reprinted with permission.*)

PART 3

Portfolio Selection

Part 3 will teach you how to implement the investment strategy you developed in Part 1 by choosing a portfolio of mutual funds suited to your needs and preferences. In Chapter 5 you will learn how to construct a portfolio of mutual funds; in Chapter 6 you will learn how to select funds for a low-risk portfolio.

Chapter 7 focuses on selecting funds for a high-growth portfolio and Chapter 8 on selecting funds for a high-income portfolio. In Chapter 9 you will learn how to select funds for a high-tax-avoidance portfolio. Finally, Chapter 10 will illustrate how to use portfolio selection to implement an investment plan.

5

Constructing a
Portfolio of
Mutual Funds

In this chapter you will learn about the principles behind construction of portfolios and the reasons why you should construct a portfolio of funds.

How Do You Construct a
Portfolio of Mutual Funds?

Completing the worksheets that help you to define your investment objectives brings you to the point where you must consider how to construct portfolios of mutual funds that will meet your individual objectives. The next several chapters are going to deal with the problem of how to construct appropriate portfolios of funds based on these results.

Before beginning to construct specific portfolios, some general discussion of the basic principles involved in producing appropriate portfolios is in order. The following chapters of the book will discuss such questions as:

Why construct portfolios?

What needs to be considered in constructing a portfolio?

What else, besides funds, should be in the portfolio and in what proportion?

How do you select the specific funds to compose your portfolio?

How do you use the information you have developed about your individual situation in constructing your portfolio?

How often should you reconsider your portfolio?

Mutual funds are themselves portfolios. They consist of a carefully chosen selection of stocks and other investments that in the best judgment of the fund's managers will achieve the fund's objectives as nearly as possible. The portfolio of securities that makes up a mutual fund is constructed and managed by the managers of the fund using whatever techniques they may know about and be comfortable about using. These techniques often include complex mathematical methods for evaluating the characteristics of the fund such as those for which the 1990 Nobel Memorial Prize in Economic Science was (in part) awarded. The three winners, Harry M. Markowitz, Merton H. Miller, and William F. Sharpe, have been called "the intellectual fathers of the mutual fund business"[1] because their mathematical analysis has found wide application in planning mutual fund portfolios.

Such techniques, although invaluable to mutual fund managers and other institutional investors, are beyond the scope of this book and too complex for use by the average individual investor. But one key concept that has grown out of these Nobel Laureates' work and is widely used on Wall Street can also be used by noninstitutional investors. It is the concept that numbers called *betas* (from the name of the second letter of the Greek alphabet) be used to compare the riskiness of holding particular stocks or funds as compared to the inherent riskiness of the market as a whole. Betas are simple enough to be used by the individual investor and are widely published in mutual fund handbooks and other reference material.

The New York Times[2] carried an article about the 1990 economics prize to these men that remarked that "betas are widely used on

[1]Robert Litan, economist, Brookings Institute, as reported in *The New York Times*, October 17, 1990, p. D-1.

[2]Peter Passell, "Ideas That Changed Wall Street and Fathered Mutual Funds," *The New York Times*, October 17, 1990, pp. D1, D6.

Wall Street (and ignored by less sophisticated investors at the peril of their purses)." Betas measure how one stock, or group of stocks, will be likely to fare relative to the stock market as a whole. A stock (or fund) with a beta equal to 1.0 will be likely to go up or down as much as the stock market as a whole. One with a beta of 1.4 would be likely to go up or down by 40 percent more than the corresponding move in the stock market. A beta lower than 1.0 means that the security moves less strongly than the market. Negative betas indicate that the security tends to move in the opposite direction from the market. When the market drops, the stock tends to rise and vice versa.

You might expect that you should select the outstanding fund of the type you have decided you need to invest in to meet your particular investment objectives and use all your available investment money to buy shares of that fund. This would, indeed, be a good strategy for allocating your investment funds if you could foresee what the financial markets and your fund in particular would do over the relevant period. Since no one can reliably predict the future, either in general or for specific markets, investors are advised to put their money in more than one fund to increase the chances that at least some money will be in a fund that will approximately meet their objectives. The exact number of funds to be selected will depend on the amount of money to be invested, the number of desirable funds that exist with the proper characteristics, and the personal preferences of the investor.

If you have only a very small amount of money to invest, you may have no choice but to pick one fund with a low minimum investment and put all your money in that fund. If you have a larger amount to invest, you may want to choose several funds and spread your investment money around among these funds. For example, if you are investing $20,000 you might choose four or five funds. For larger amounts you might choose even more funds.

Overall Allocation of Your Investment Funds

There are many possible strategies for allocating investment funds in a portfolio and many sources of advice about allocation that you could use to supplement this book. The allocation of your investment funds among different investments is constantly subject to reevaluation as changing conditions warrant revision.

Financial publications such as *The Wall Street Journal, Barron's, Fortune, Money,* newsletters about investing, and many others give timely information for planning the proper proportions of investments for your portfolio. Other sources include financial broadcasts such as "Wall Street Week," "Adam Smith's Money World," or numerous broadcasts on the Financial News Network. By getting up-to-date opinions and facts from sources such as these and combining such input with your own judgment about current and future economic and market prospects, you can use the principles outlined in this book to allocate your investment funds to appropriate types of investments and then use the procedures detailed in the following chapters to select specific funds for your individual investment categories.

You will probably want your investment portfolio to include some cash or cash equivalents, such as money market funds, U.S Treasury securities, or an insured savings account, in order to give you some liquidity for purchases as opportunities arise. You may possibly want some investments which are not expected to grow extremely rapidly but can be expected to produce substantial amounts of income (possibly including utility bonds, stocks, or annuities). If you feel strongly that you want some other type of asset (gold, for example), you could include a small percentage of that type. Then your remaining assets would be allocated to the mutual funds that you select. There will be more discussion about how to select these funds in the following chapters.

As an example, a fairly conservative portfolio might have a distribution of assets that looks somewhat as follows:

Money market funds	40%
Income funds	20%
Low-risk stock funds	40%

You could be less conservative by picking more aggressive funds or by increasing the percentage devoted to stock funds. You could increase your allocation to fixed-income securities when interest rates are high and buying opportunities are rare in order to benefit from the high rates. You could buy bond funds when interest rates are high and you expect them to drop, in order to benefit from the rise in value of the bonds. In any event, you should frequently reconsider your allocation to reflect changing economic conditions or your changing lifestyle or stage of life. Managing your portfolio is an active process that should be reconsidered frequently.

Alternatively you could consider buying funds which reallocate assets for you (asset allocation funds or balanced funds) or pick an asset allocation formula you feel comfortable with and stick to it. For example a young person trying for long-term growth might decide to keep 10 percent in cash and put the rest in growth funds; someone with a more conservative outlook might put 50 percent in growth funds and 50 percent in money market funds. The point of this strategy is that over a long period you do not want to try to anticipate all the gyrations of the market. This approach may reduce your return somewhat, but it will relieve you of the burden of anticipating economic change and reallocating your portfolio appropriately when change occurs.

The following chapters will discuss in more detail how you determine the specific funds to include in your portfolio.

If some of this part's chapters are less relevant to your needs than others, skip to the chapter summaries at the end and concentrate on the chapters that interest you more.

6
Low-Risk Portfolios

In this chapter you will learn about portfolios where low risk is the most important consideration. You will also learn how to select funds for such a portfolio.

What Does Risk Mean?

Most people have some idea of what risk is. A common reaction might be that risk is something that is "chancy" or that involves danger. Risk is present when something bad might happen. There are certain activities that most people would regard as risky, such as sky diving, driving racing cars, or flying hang gliders. Although these may indeed be risky activities, often people's perceptions of risk are distorted or exaggerated. Many people perceive the risk of being killed by terrorists as a major danger in foreign travel, when in fact statistics show that the level of risk is actually very small. Although terrorist incidents get a great deal of attention, they are relatively few in number, and the number of people who travel abroad without incident is large.

The study of risks is one of the tasks pursued by actuaries and some related professions. The following list from *Science 85* magazine (October 1985, p. 41, reprinted by permission of the author, William F. Allman) demonstrates the actual incidence of some selected categories of risk expressed in terms of days of life lost for each activity—for example, being an unmarried male takes about 10 years off the expected life span:

Risk	Days lost
Being an unmarried male	3500
Smoking cigarettes and being male	2250
Heart disease	2100
Being an unmarried female	1600
Being 30% overweight	1300
Being a coal miner	1100
Cancer	980
Being 20% overweight	900
Having less than an 8th grade education	850
Smoking cigarettes and being female	800
Being poor	700
Stroke	520
Driving a motor vehicle	207
Accidents in the home	95
Suicide	95
Being murdered	90
Walking down the street	37
Natural radiation	8
Medical X rays	6
Drinking diet sodas	2
Radiation from the nuclear industry	0.02

SOURCE: William F. Allman, "The Compleat Worrier," *Science 85,* October 1985, p. 41.

It is apparent that the perceived risk is often much different than the real risk. This is also true in relation to economics, investing, and other areas of personal finance. For example, most people do not appreciate that the real risk of suffering a loss of income which materially affects your standard of living over the next 10 years is one chance in four.

For investing, the term *risk* takes on a little different connotation. Here risk is generally understood to mean the probability of loss. A risky investment is therefore an investment with a relatively high probability that you might lose all or some of the money you have invested. A safe, or low-risk, investment on the other hand is an investment that has little chance of resulting in loss for the investor.

Loss, like risk, can take different forms. Investors can lose their money because they invested in what turned out to be a bad choice of companies (i.e., the company stops growing as expected, faces new competition or a new technology that wipes out its competitive advantage, or the manager who created its success resigns or dies or retires), or because the markets crashed as a result of economic or political considerations that undermine investors' confidence. An investor might also lose because of inflation, even though the investment appeared to be successful (the investment went up in value but was worth less than the initial money invested after adjusting for inflation).

Closely related to the concept of risk is the concept of volatility. *Volatility* refers to the extent of up and down fluctuation in the value of the investment. A federally insured certificate of deposit from a bank has essentially no volatility. The amount to be paid is guaranteed to be as stated at the time that the CD matures. Similarly, a passbook savings account builds up in a manner prescribed by the bank for that type of account and does not change as a result of market fluctuations or other factors.

However, a security that can be resold to another investor, even a very safe security such as a short-term government one (a Treasury bill for example) will fluctuate at least a little in value in response to market conditions, especially interest rates. Although the price may fluctuate, the security will eventually be paid at a definite price, so the range of fluctuation will depend strongly on the amount of time that remains before the security matures. Someone who purchases the security knows that it will have a definite redemption value on a certain specific date. As that date approaches, the market price will tend to approach the redemption value.

A short-term security (or a long-term security nearing its redemption date) will generally tend to sell for a price approaching its redemption price unless there is doubt that the issuer will be able to pay the redemption amount when due. That is why very short term securities tend to have little risk if the issuer is sound and able to pay. Even the market fluctuations tend to have diminished impact as the payoff day approaches, since the payoff value sets the ultimate price for the security. If the price gets too high or too low relative to the approaching payoff, the investors will tend to bid it up or down to a price more in line with the current interest rates.

Although volatility and risk are related, they are not identical. Investments with low volatility and low risk include bank deposits or certain stocks that pay a generous dividend. These investments tend not to fluctuate much in price and have traditionally been described as appropriate for widows and orphans, because unsophisticated investors could be confident that their money would be safe in such investments.

Any consideration of how risky an investment is or how appropriate a certain degree of risk is for a certain portfolio must consider the period involved. In general, the longer the time during which the investor expects to leave the money invested, the more risk the investor could consider accepting, all other things being equal. This is true because the stock market has a very good record of providing good returns to investors over a long time, but it can fluctuate strongly either up or down over shorter periods. A good rule of thumb for an investor is that he or she must be prepared to sustain a 30 percent drop in the value of his or her investment in any given year, but that the market nearly always recoups the loss within 12 to 18 months. The greatest danger is that the invested money will be needed during a downturn and have to be cashed in at a substantial loss. For example, you invest $5000 that you expect to use later toward a down payment on a new house. Assume also that a few months later you find the house that you want to buy, but your $5000 has now dwindled to $3000. If you could wait for a year or two your investment might recover and show a profit, but if you need the money now you might have to take a 40 percent loss.

However, a young college graduate investing money for a retirement fund or a grandparent investing for college or money to start a business for a newly born grandchild has a long enough time horizon to invest in somewhat aggressive investments. A 64-year-old investing for retirement in a year or two should stick to nonvolatile investments.

The keys to dealing with risk in investment are to:

1. Understand how risk originates
2. Understand how risk relates to return
3. Understand the impact that risk has on your investments in the time frame under consideration
4. Understand how diversification can reduce the effect of risk on your investments

It is important to recognize that although risk is often discussed as though it were a single entity, it can arise from many sources including:

Market risk

Company financial risk

Geographical risk (or country risk)

Industry risk

Political risk

The impact of risk can be diminished by diversifying. Consider a simple example. Assume that you run a small insurance company. If you insure most of the people in one small town and the town is struck by an epidemic of serious disease, your company could be in serious financial trouble. However, if you were careful to diversify your portfolio of insurance coverage by limiting the number of policies in any one town to a small percentage of the town's population, you would barely be affected.

When Risk Is the Most Important Consideration

The premise of this chapter is that risk counts most for people who do not want to take risk. These risk-averse investors are less concerned about getting a high return than about avoiding loss of their investment capital. In the rest of this chapter we will present a strategy for constructing portfolios primarily of no-load mutual funds that consider risk as the most important factor. These portfolios will recognize that for the investor concerned primarily about risk, the low-risk category is the most important. This is because few investors attempt to find high-risk investments because they are high risk. To the extent that investors are interested in high-risk investments, they are looking for high return and are aware that high risk frequently accompanies high return. Our low-risk portfolio discussion will also consider income, growth, and tax avoidance as secondary characteristics of these portfolios. Before launching into this discussion, it is important to recognize that there are many facets of risk influencing these recommendations.

One area of consideration that affects choices you should make is your assessment of the future general direction of movements in the economy and the stock and bond markets. These assessments have critical implications for the context and meaning of the term *risk* as it applies to your actions at the time you are making your investment decisions, and these implications have to be considered in determining the proper allocation of your investment assets among the various types of investments. For purposes of this book, the investment assets will be primarily no-load mutual funds, and the allocation question addressed in this chapter will be how to allocate investment funds among no-load mutual funds to achieve an appropriate degree of risk (low) and some appropriate level of the secondary characteristics desired by the investor. Later in the chapter we will construct some sample portfolios and describe some general principles for constructing portfolios with the detailed characteristics for the situation where risk is the overriding concern.

Although we will be presenting some sample portfolios for certain types of situations, remember that any samples have to be adjusted to reflect your needs and the current situation as you perceive it. If the stock market is generally rising, for example, and if you expect it to continue rising for the foreseeable future, you may want to shift a small percentage of your low-risk assets to relatively safe equity funds such as funds that invest primarily in high-quality blue chip stocks. This would increase your investment risk somewhat but would tend to raise your investment return and help offset the risk of inflation.

However, in a situation where you anticipate that the markets will be falling, the low-risk portfolio owner may want to shift more assets into cash and cash equivalents such as money market funds or short-term government securities (such as Treasury bills and Treasury certificates). This is especially true if the portfolio needs to provide liquid assets.

Of course it is not your perception of the economic climate that will affect the performance of your portfolio, it is the actual performance of the economy and, specifically, the markets, that will ultimately count. But since you must make your evaluation of what is appropriate before you know what will really happen, you can only base your portfolio on your own judgment, guided by whatever publications and economic forecasts you choose to consider in your analysis. Portfolio strategy techniques such as those treated in this chapter can never hope to reflect all the relevant considerations. These techniques should not be viewed as a cookbook for constructing portfolios but rather as a beginning for all the considerations that should enter into your evaluation. In addition to the general economic climate, as you perceive it to be, many other factors may affect your investment results. Just a few of these include:

Technological change

Political change or instability (threats of war, ideological change, etc.)

Seasonality and other cyclical factors

Taxation

Debt-rating changes (especially as they reflect actual or perceived deterioration in the financial strength of companies)

Changes in supply and demand for a product or commodity

Asset quality deterioration in the companies in which you have invested (possibly for one of the reasons shown elsewhere on this list)

Capital flight from a geographical area

Market instability (program trading, junk bond defaults, etc.)

Major institutional bankruptcies and financial weakness (S&Ls, banks, insurance companies, etc.)

Interest rate trends

Government policies (fiscal policies, Federal Reserve action, etc.)

For low-risk portfolios, *caution* is the watchword. In addition to using low-risk strategies for designing your portfolio, you should consider how to use your best judgment to weigh these and many other relevant factors starting with the guidelines in this chapter and adding your own evaluation to adjust the results.

Portfolio Examples

The basic principles of portfolio construction were discussed in general terms at the beginning of Part 3. The rest of Chapter 6 will present in some detail the step-by-step instructions and specific sample portfolios that might have been constructed to meet the needs of particular investors. For example, the first group of examples to follow will deal with how to create low-risk portfolios. Markets and related factors are constantly changing so that portfolios that are appropriate for a particular situation are constantly subject to change. Indeed, what is appropriate can change from day to day if a major change in the relevant factors occurs (a war breaks out, a major breakthrough is announced in science or medicine, etc.).

In order to give you specific examples, this book assumes that you will use the latest currently available information. You can use this information to produce a portfolio of funds that meets your individual needs. A practical approach provides worksheets for you to produce your own portfolio. No esoteric mathematics or complex knowledge of the financial markets are required. Our method is simple enough and practical enough that anyone who is willing to put in a little effort can produce a portfolio that will meet his or her investment objectives.

The method relies on reviewing the recent performance of funds as published in any of the numerous lists of mutual funds published in financial publications and filtering out ones that have appropriate performance on the four key measures that have previously been discussed (risk, growth, income, and tax avoidance).

You have previously determined which of these factors are most important to you (for example: risk first, followed by growth, followed by income, followed by tax avoidance), so potentially there are a large number of possible portfolios (risk, growth, income, tax avoidance; risk, growth, tax avoidance, income; etc.). We have simplified that list by assuming that the first two categories are the most important and the only ones that need to be addressed at this stage of portfolio planning. We also assume that some categories are not desirable in themselves and so do not need to be considered as primary choices. For example, it is difficult to conceive of an investor whose primary portfolio objective would be to achieve high risk. More likely, investors who accept high risk do so because they recognize the need to accept some additional risk in order to get higher returns. Consequently, we do not present a portfolio where the primary aim is high risk or one with the primary aim of low tax avoidance.

Although the portfolios presented are based on historical data, it should be obvious by now that these are not presented as portfolios for the reader to choose at the time he or she reads the book but rather are intended as examples of *how to use the method.* You should read these examples for an explanation of how to construct a portfolio that meets your own needs and then use currently available sources plus other knowledge gained from reading, broadcasts, and your own insights as input to an individualized portfolio.

The portfolio selection approach discussed here assumes that you are faced with a research problem: how to find and evaluate information about mutual funds available for investment. The first step in the approach is to look for publicly available, unbiased, and reliable sources of information that are intelligible to a person who is a layperson in the investments area. From these sources, you are advised to select an array of funds which are suitable for the investment strategy developed as a result of self-assessment exercises in Chapters 2 and 3. Then methods for evaluating and comparing the funds included in the array are applied in order to choose those that are best for your purposes from among them.

Three portfolios will be considered in Part 3:

Low-risk and moderate growth

Low-risk and moderate income

Low-risk and moderate tax avoidance

The method for choosing which mutual funds will be included will be the same in all cases. A process for selecting funds to represent growth, income, and tax avoidance from publicly available sources will be presented and illustrated by examples.

Low Risk and Moderate Growth

Asset allocation recommendations for this category usually amount to the following: *Keep a percentage of your assets in cash (how much depends on general economic and market conditions you perceive or expect) and divide the balance evenly between stocks and bonds.* Another option which captures the spirit of this type of recommendation is to invest in funds which have the objective of investing in both growth and income securities in a "balanced" approach. If you elect to invest in balanced funds, then you are relying on the funds' managements to choose a proper asset allocation strategy.

Balanced Funds—A Sample of Choices.   In this example you will see an approach which will be repeated in subsequent illustrations of portfolio selection:

1. The first step is to define the type of mutual fund that interests you, in this case, a balanced fund.

2. The second step is to find a publicly available source of information which lists ratings of this type of fund and was published more than 2 years ago (but less than 3 years ago), assuming a certain amount of market stability during recent times.

In this example, the source for this step was *Business Week*'s list, published February 22, 1988, under the title "Mutual Fund Scoreboard," which follows an article entitled "The Best Mutual Funds." The article lists 25 "Top Performers," of which the following five are described as being very low risk balanced funds:

Dodge and Cox Balanced

Fidelity Puritan

Phoenix Balanced

Strong Investment

Wellington

When you examine these funds in the "Mutual Fund Scoreboard," you find that Phoenix has an 8.5 percent sales charge, Dodge and Cox and Wellington are no-loads, Fidelity Puritan charges 2 percent, and Strong Investment has a 1 percent load. However you also find that Strong has had high portfolio turnover and had 86 percent of its assets in cash, quite different from Dodge and Cox, Wellington, or Fidelity Puritan.

In step 2 you have found three possibilities that look good:

Dodge and Cox: 5-year average annual return is 15.7 percent

Fidelity Puritan: 5-year average annual return is 16.2 percent

Wellington: 5-year average annual return is 16.3 percent

You have found one questionable fund:

Strong Investment: 5-year average annual return is 17.4 percent

You have found one high-performing *load fund* (to probably eliminate):

Phoenix Balanced: 5-year average annual return is 18.1 percent

3. In the third step, find other public sources of ratings, published within the last year, preferably different from the source you used in step 2.

To illustrate step 3, we will use mutual funds data from *Consumer Reports, Money, Forbes,* and *Barron's.*[1] First look for a current assessment of the Strong Investment Fund to decide whether you should consider or eliminate this fund as a possible choice.

In *Money's* listing, Strong Investment's performance is rated D, with F the only lower rating; A, B, and C are possible higher ratings. However, *Consumer Reports* rates the relative risk of Strong Investment as best on its 5-point scale in comparison to average stock market losses during two difficult periods—8/21/87 to 12/4/87 and 10/6/89 to 10/13/89. *Forbes* gives Strong Investment an A rating for "down" markets and a D rating for "up" markets. In *Barron's,* Strong Investment's return on a 5-year initial investment of $10,000 (9/30/85 to 9/30/90) is given as $15,988.50 (i.e., an initial investment of $10,000 on 9/30/85 would have grown to $15,988.50 on 9/30/90). Compare this to *Barron's* February 15, 1988, issue, which shows a $22,323.90 return for 12/31/82 to 12/31/87.

It is clear from this review that Strong Investment may still be a low-risk fund, although we may have some questions about how its historical performance compares with other low-risk funds to be considered next in the analysis. So it is not a good idea to eliminate this choice. We have to look further.

The Dodge and Cox Balanced fund is not included in *Money, Consumer Reports,* or *Forbes* listings. *Barron's* indicates a 5-year return of $18,793.80 (9/30/85 to 9/30/90) compared to $20,818.30 (12/31/82 to 12/31/87), which suggests a more stable record of performance than Strong Investment Fund.

Fidelity Puritan captures an A from *Money,* and *Consumer Reports*

---

[1]"Mutual Funds 1990, Part 1," *Consumer Reports,* May 1990; "The Alphabetical Guide to 960 Mutual Funds," *Money,* February 1990; "Annual Fund Ratings," *Forbes,* September 3, 1990; and "Lipper Gauge,"*Barron's,* mutual funds quarterly listing, November 12, 1990 (and February 15, 1988).

rates this fund a better-than-average relative risk for 8/21/87 to 12/4/87 and a best relative risk for 10/6/89 to 10/13/89. *Forbes* characterizes Fidelity Puritan as a B in both "up" and "down" markets. *Barron's* reports a 5-year return on an initial $10,000 investment as $16,167.60 (9/30/85 to 9/30/90) in comparison to $21,246.60 (12/31/82 to 12/32/87). This range is rather similar to the one for the Strong Investment Fund.

The Wellington Fund (Vanguard) was rated B by *Money*. *Consumer Reports'* relative risk ratings were the same as for Fidelity Puritan—better than average and best relative to the stock market during two downturns. *Forbes* considers Wellington Fund an A in "up" and a C in "down" markets. *Barron's* reported the 5-year return on an initial $10,000 investment as $17,431.10 (9/30/85 to 9/30/90) compared to $21,291.30 (12/31/82 to 12/32/87).

Considering these four possibilities as choices, Dodge and Cox Balanced Fund looks tempting in terms of most recent 5-year performance. However, so far you have the least expert guidance available about this fund from public sources, probably because this is the smallest of the four in terms of assets (only $63.5 million). Further scrutiny and research would be appropriate before deciding on this fund.

The other three possibilities, Strong Investment, Fidelity Puritan, and Wellington, appear to be roughly similar. Of the three, Wellington might be best in terms of recent performance and sales charges. Here too, you might want to conduct additional research before investing your money in any of these funds. Also, as in the case of any fund, you should read the prospectus carefully before investing. (An example of additional research is provided by Figure 6-1. Does this figure influence your opinion about Strong Investment?)

In Figure 6-1 you see a smoothed graph of a measure of fund performance for four mutual funds. The performance measure plotted here is return on initial $10,000 investment after 5 years. This measure represents the total present value of an investment of $10,000 in the fund made 5 years prior to the date for which the measure is reported. For example, for fourth quarter 1987, return on initial $10,000 investment after 5 years for any fund reflects the value as of 12/31/87 of a $10,000 investment made on 12/31/82. Investment value is calculated under the assumptions that all dividends and gains have been reinvested and that no taxes are deducted. In this graph, the points do not all fall on the plotted lines because the plots are "smoothed" to show trends

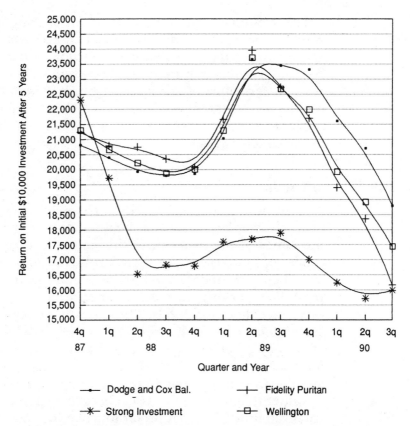

Figure 6-1. Low-risk balanced fund trends for 3 years (return on initial $10,000 investment after 5 years).

more clearly. That means the lines shown are plotted according to an equation which takes into account the relationship among the points and presents an idealized picture of that relationship.

A graph which compares fund performance using the measure we have chosen gives us a picture of long-term trends mapped during a specific period, in this case, over 12 quarters from 1987 to 1990. What we see in Figure 6-1 is that three of the funds track each other rather nicely, but a fourth, Strong Investment, shows a different pattern of long-term performance. Strong's long-term performance declined very rapidly during the period following the 1987 stock market crash. The other funds were far less affected. After this decline, Strong's performance stabilized at a much lower level. Although the other funds were more variable in their postcrash performance, they continued to exceed Strong's performance, even after a long decline beginning in mid-1989.

This example provided guidance for seeking information on which to base a decision. The actual choices which will confront you if you attempt to construct a portfolio such as this with low risk and a moderately high rate of growth will depend on the recent performance of the relevant funds as well as other factors which have been discussed. Your final choices should reflect careful consideration of all the contextual factors referred to earlier in the chapter as well.

Low-Risk Growth Funds

The previous example focused on balanced funds for a portfolio with relatively low risk where the asset allocation decision is left in the hands of the manager of the funds—managers of balanced funds continuously adjust their fund's allocation of assets in line with their assessment of the many relevant factors that affect the portfolio's performance. A similar approach could also be used with asset allocation funds. These relatively new funds make the asset allocation decision for you as well. Asset allocation funds allow for a greater range of variation in the asset allocations than do balanced funds, which adjust their holdings between growth and income within a relatively narrow range of securities.

Rather than leaving the asset allocation choices to managers of balanced funds, you may prefer to make your own asset allocation decisions, you may prefer to use the 50/50% rule suggested at the beginning of this section, or you may want to choose some other percentages based on your own judgment or on the opinions of experts whose views you respect (as expressed in business publications, newsletters, or broadcasts). In any event, if you want to choose growth funds using such an approach, the following example (low-risk growth funds) may be helpful. This will be followed by a section on choosing low-risk portfolios that yield a moderate level of income using income funds.

The steps to be followed using your own asset allocation scheme and a portfolio of (relatively low-risk) growth mutual funds to construct a low-risk portfolio are similar to the steps in the example for balanced funds.

1. Define the type of fund under consideration—low-risk growth funds.

2. Choose current sources of published data to evaluate risk and performance. In this example, we will make our first selection

based on current information and work back in time to assess the performance stability of the funds under consideration.

To proceed with the illustration of step 2, the *Consumer Reports* listing used previously will again be used to make the first choices. This is a portfolio where low risk is the primary consideration, so the procedure starts with stock funds that have been rated as having very low risk. Of the funds rated "best" in this list in terms of relative risk (i.e., how much this fund goes up or down relative to market changes—a concept closely related to the numerical rating of risk known as "beta") for the two time periods being considered, only two are growth funds. The others are either balanced funds or income funds. This is not terribly surprising, since you know that you may have to give up some growth to achieve lower risk. The two funds are the Mathers Growth fund and the Lindner Growth fund. But if you are willing to move down in the relative risk category from "best" to "better than average" for the 8/21/87 to 12/4/87 period (while still including only funds that were rated "best" for the 10/6/89 to 10/23/89 period), you add one additional fund, the Nicholas Growth fund. All three funds are no-load. Table 6-1 compares the three funds based on data from an investor's guide. In addition, *Money* gave all three funds a B rating; *Forbes* rates Mathers C in both "up" and "down" markets and rates Lindner Growth and Income as a D in "up" markets and an A+ in "down" markets. Nicholas Growth was rated C in "up" markets and "A" in "down" markets by *Forbes*.

Table 6-1. Fund Comparison

Fund	5-year annual return, %	Total risk rank	Risk-adjusted return	Bull market return, %	Bear market return, %	Market risk beta
Mathers	18 (high)	Average	Above average	25.6 (average)	3.7 (average)	0.57
Lindner	16.7 (above average)	Average	Above average	45.9 (above average)	14.9 (average)	0.61
Nicholas	16 (above average)	Average	Average	46.9 (above average)	−19.1 (below average)	0.71

Adapted from *The Individual Investor's Guide to No-Load Mutual Funds* (9th ed.), American Association of Individual Investors, with permission.

3. Looking back to *Business Week*'s 1988 listing, Lindner Growth and Income received the highest performance rating, Mathers was characterized as "average," and Nicholas as "just above average." In the *Business Week* listing, Lindner is reported to be "very low risk," Mathers is called "average risk," and Nicholas is "low risk."

Comparing this to the *Barron's* lists dated 2/15/88 and 11/12/90 for return on an initial investment of $10,000 we get:

	12/31/82 to 12/31/87	9/30/85 to 9/30/90
Lindner	$20,861.20	$17,321.10
Mathers	20,878.00	22,703.80
Nicholas	19,610.80	15,345.40

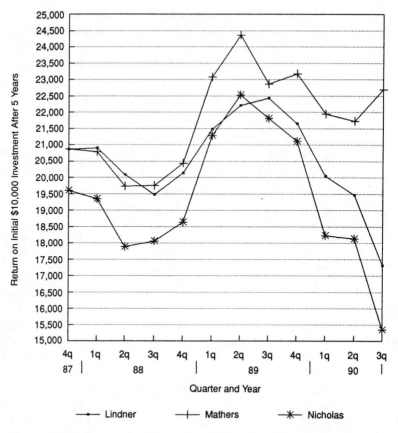

Figure 6-2. Low-risk growth fund trends for 3 years (return on initial investment after 5 years).

From this table it looks clear that the Mathers fund has done substantially better than the other two in the most recent period despite the nearly equivalent performance of the three funds in the earlier period. Figure 6-2 plots these results in order to verify that there is really a pattern of difference. This point-to-point chart of performance could be produced by hand on graph paper and serves to display the trends rather well. An improved version (Figure 6-3) has been produced using graphics software which fits a smooth curve to the data points. Although the interpretation of both charts is identical, it is easier to see the trends with the software-produced charts, which will be used throughout the remainder of this book.

As you can see, Mathers appears to be a clearly superior choice among these three funds. The other funds are dropping off while

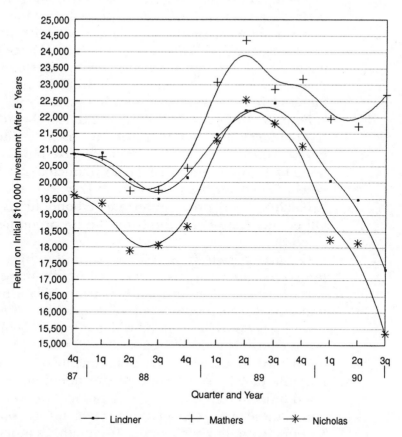

Figure 6-3. Smoothed curves for low-risk growth fund trends for 3 years.

Mathers has declined less rapidly in the past and is now improving.

Low Risk and Moderate Income

Since the second most important investment feature selected in this category is income, asset allocation would tend to heavily favor income funds. In this section we will apply again the methods discussed up to this point.

Step 1.   To increase the range of choices, this step will include initial prospective and retrospective selections, combining the approaches used in the two previous examples. In addition, a load fund will be included in this illustration because its performance record is instructive.

When you examine *Business Week*'s 1988 listing of top stock fund performers, only two possibilities offered have income as their objective, and they are both characterized as very low risk: Eaton Vance Income-Boston and Wellesley Income. Eaton Vance Income-Boston imposes a sales charge and had 3 percent of assets in Pennsylvania Power and Light at the end of 1987. Wellesley Income is a no-load fund which had 2 percent of assets in Pacific Corp.

Business Week's 2/29/88 Bond Fund Scoreboard lists only one "corporate-quality" bond fund among eighteen cited for superior performance. This is the Vanguard Fixed-Income Short-Term bond fund. Although three quality municipal funds are listed (to be considered in the next section "Low Risk and Moderate Tax Avoidance"), no other government bond funds are included. Other corporate bond funds on the list are either "general" or "high-yield."

Consumer Reports' June 1990 bond fund ratings defined risk in terms of a comparison between each fund's monthly total return and the return on three-month Treasury bills. Under this definition only two corporate bond funds qualify as "best" risks: (1) T. Rowe Price-Short-Term Bond with a portfolio quality of A and an average maturity of 1.8 years and (2) Vanguard Fixed-Income Short-Term Bond with a portfolio quality of AA and an average maturity of 2.3 years. None of the nonmunicipal government bond funds received a "best" risk rating. Five were "better" risks, and of these only one had an average maturity comparable to the corporate funds cited above: Twentieth Century U.S. Governments with a portfolio quality of AAA and an average maturity of 3.2 years.

Consumer Reports' 1990 stock fund listing includes several "best risk for 2 periods" income funds. These are:

Wellesley Income

Stein-Roe Total Return

USAA Mutual Income

Burnham

Lindner Dividend

Permanent Portfolio

At this point it is important to recognize that only Wellesley Income and Vanguard Fixed-Income Short-Term Bond are common to both *Business Week* 1988 and *Consumer Reports* 1990. What do other sources have to say about these two possibilities? Wellesley Income gets an A rating from *Money;* *Forbes* gives it a D in "up" markets and an A+ in "down" markets. Vanguard Fixed-Income Short-Term Bond is not rated by *Money;* *Forbes* gives this fund a C in "up" markets and a D in "down" markets.

Step 2.   In our analysis we will first compare Wellesley and Vanguard Fixed-Income to three competitors: Eaton Vance Income-Boston, T. Rowe Price Short-Term Bond, and Twentieth Century-U.S. Government. Then we will examine the remaining comparisons which arise from the *Consumer Reports* stock fund listing.

Figure 6-4 shows performance for 3 years of the above in terms of return on an initial $10,000 investment. The results indicate a consistent pattern of superior and stable performance by Vanguard in relation to two other bond funds. Wellesley had the best performance but within a much wider band of variation. Eaton-Vance appears to be plummeting off the chart and would be eliminated from consideration by the direction taken. Sales charges connected with this load fund would support such a decision.

Figure 6-5 shows the comparative performance of Vanguard Fixed-Income Short-Term Bond and Wellesley Income in relation to the "best" risk stock income funds selected from *Consumer Re-*

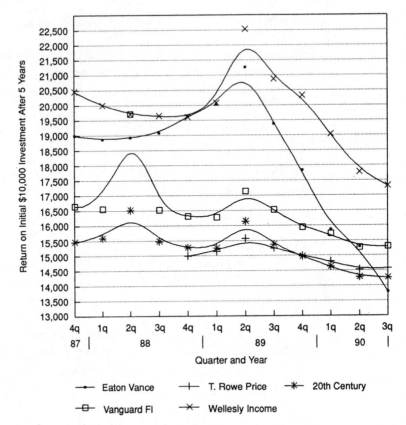

Figure 6-4. Low-risk income fund trends for 3 years (return on initial $10,000 investment after 5 years).

ports' 1990 listing. In this second comparison, Lindner Dividend is relatively stable and follows the Wellesley Income trend, except at a lower level of performance. Burnham is almost identical to Stein-Roe Total Return but offers the highest performance levels and high overall variation in performance. From the point of view of performance stability, Lindner dividend, Wellesley, and Vanguard Fixed-Income Short-Term Bond funds appear to be most attractive in this grouping, which is less stable overall than the first group of income funds compared in the preceding figure.

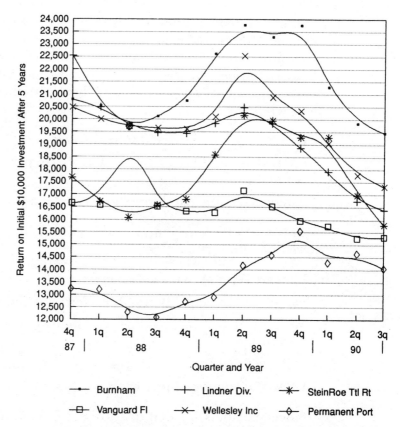

Figure 6-5. Vanguard and Wellesley Funds compared with "best" risk income funds (return on initial $10,000 investment after 5 years.

Low Risk and Moderate
Tax Avoidance

All the funds considered in this section are similar in several respects:

1. They are all municipal bond funds without state geographical limitations.

2. All the funds have portfolios of very short maturity—2.7 years or less (or 4.7 years in one case).

3. All receive *Forbes'* lowest performance rating in "up" markets, and all receive *Forbes'* highest rating in "down" markets (or next to highest in one case).

One may readily understand from the above commonalities why these funds qualify for this category of portfolio. The choices were made from the same sources referenced in previous sections. In *Business Week*'s 2/29/88 bond fund listing only three municipal-quality funds are among those with the highest performance ratings:

Calvert Tax Free Reserve-Limited (no load)

Limited-Term Municipal (sales fee of 2.75 percent and an average maturity of 4.7 years)

Vanguard Municipal Bond Short-Term (no load)

In *Consumer Reports'* June 1990 bond fund listing, five funds received the "best" risk rating:

Limited Term Municipal (as above)

Vanguard Municipal Bond Short-Term (as above)

Merrill Lynch Municipal Limited Maturity (sales charge of 0.75 percent)

T. Rowe Price Tax Free Short-Intermediate (no load)

USAA Tax Exempt Short-Term (no load)

Since six funds in total are to be considered, including two mentioned by both sources, Figure 6-6 compares their 3-year performance simultaneously. The performance measure offered by *Barron's* municipal bond fund listings provides a percentage change attributable to reinvestment over 5 years as a yardstick that is equivalent to the 5-year total return in dollars used to gauge performance of other mutual funds. Unfortunately, this measure is not directly comparable, and these funds have to be set apart as a unique and different class of investments in our consideration, because we do not have the means of comparing them to other mutual funds in our analysis.*

The initial impression created by Figure 6-6 is that the Limited Term performance is well worth the sales fee and additional level of instability associated with it. Among the other funds represented, the pattern of performance is very similar, but performance levels appear to be higher for Calvert and USAA consistently over the 2-year period for which data were published in *Barron's*.

---

*After this was written, *Barron's* revised this performance measure to make it equivalent to performance measures of other mutual funds.

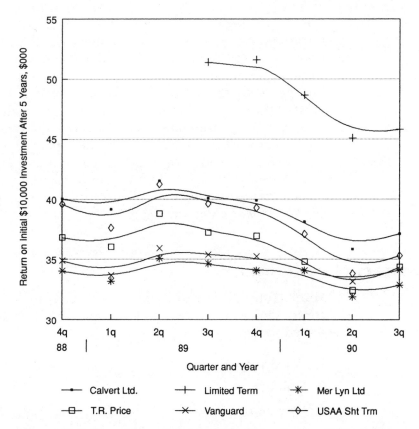

Figure 6-6. Low-risk municipal fund trends for 2 years (total reinvestment percentage change over 5 years.

Warning: Read before
Summary of Performance

To a large extent, our analysis has relied on the publicly reported judgments of experts and visual impressions created by graphic performance trend comparisons. In this section we will describe a simple analysis that highlights features of mutual fund performance which supplement the results of graphical presentation. However, if you prefer to avoid doing arithmetic, it is entirely appropriate to rely solely on the analytical approach taken up to this point, i.e., consultation with published sources and charting of graphs of performance. You do *not* have to follow through with the supplementary analysis recommended here, although it does have certain advantages that will be discussed.

For some people, especially those who are visually talented, interpretation of graphs is easy, and these people will need no additional supplement to their understanding to select the best funds from a graphic array. For others, it is not readily apparent what interpretation should be taken from charted performance. Since most of the work required to do a numerical analysis as described in this section has already been done by researching the information necessary to prepare a graph, these people may find the calculations proposed here rather useful at a cost of relatively little extra effort necessary to do these simple computations.

So if you are undaunted by arithmetic, please proceed, but *if you hate numbers, stop here.*

Summary of Performance

Mutual fund performance includes three components that are incorporated within the trend comparisons that have been presented so far:

1. Performance level
2. Stability
3. Direction

Of these three, graphic presentation most clearly describes direction of performance.

To supplement understanding of performance levels, an average over the 3-year period can be computed for each mutual fund.

Performance instability over the 12 quarters recorded by the graphs of balanced, growth, and income fund performance can be quantified by the variation in performance level during this period. If we subtract the average performance level from each quarter's performance, we obtain a measure of quarterly variation. To calculate an average quarterly variation, multiply each quarterly variation times itself, add all these, and then divide by 12, the total number of quarters. This number we call the "average quarterly variation." Next, take the square root of the average quarterly variation using the square root key ($\sqrt{}$) of any calculator. This final number may be called the performance instability of the mutual fund (statistically equivalent to the standard deviation of the fund's performance).

How to Calculate
Performance Instability

As an abbreviated example of how to compute performance insta-bility, consider the first fund in Table 6-2, T. Rowe Price Short-Term Bond. Five-year performance data were not available in *Barron's* for the first year of our analysis covering fourth quarter 1987 through third quarter 1990. For the 2 years that were avail-able, average quarterly performance for T. Rowe Price was:

4th Quarter 1988	14,992
1st Quarter 1989	15,148
2nd Quarter 1989	15,577
3rd Quarter 1989	15,252
4th Quarter 1989	14,995
1st Quarter 1990	14,803
2nd Quarter 1990	14,521
3rd Quarter 1990	14,574
Average performance	14,982

The average is obtained by dividing the total for 8 quarters by 8. To find quarterly performance variations for T. Rowe Price, sub-tract the average performance from each quarterly performance, as follows:

	Quarterly variations	Squared quarterly variation
4th Quarter 1988: 14,992 − 14,982 =	10	100
1st Quarter 1989: 15,148 − 14,982 =	166	27,556
2nd Quarter 1989: 15,577 − 14,982 =	598	357,604
3rd Quarter 1989: 15,252 − 14,982 =	270	72,900
4th Quarter 1989: 14,995 − 14,982 =	13	169
1st Quarter 1990: 14,803 − 14,982 =	−179	32,041
2nd Quarter 1990: 14,521 − 14,982 =	−461	212,521
3rd Quarter 1990: 14,574 − 14,982 =	−408	166,464
Average squared quarterly variation		108,221

Notice that some of the variations are positive and some are nega-tive. A computational device that allows you to add these, without canceling due to differences in sign, is the method of squaring, i.e., multiplying each variation times itself. When you do this all negative signs become positive. The result is shown in the right column, squared quarterly variation. You find the average by adding the total and dividing by 8.

Finally, performance instability is the square root of the average squared quarterly variation. The easiest way to do the last computation, finding a square root, is to use the square root key ($\sqrt{}$) of your calculator. In this case, the performance instability is 328. This is the lowest performance instability of all funds listed in the table. For our purposes, performance instability can be considered a synonym for risk.

When you calculate average performance and performance instability for each mutual fund under consideration, you have a powerful quantitative summary of facts that will help you pick the best funds. To apply this information as a guide to selecting funds, construct a table. In addition, you can combine both measures onto a single index that will be described next. These performance features are included in Tables 6-2 and 6-3, which summarize performance for balanced, growth, and income funds separately from municipal bond funds.

Each table shows funds arranged in ascending order of risk, lowest risk funds (least performance instability) at the beginning of each list. Although performance level also increases as you proceed down the lists, the relationship is not linear.

If we conceive of performance level as a benefit, and performance instability as a cost, we may ask if there is a means of comparing change in performance level to change in performance instability as our eyes descend the list. This comparison is the subject of the column for risk-adjusted performance index.

In Table 6-2, the risk-adjusted performance index indicates how much benefit is obtained in increased performance level dollars for each "cost" dollar of performance instability increase when each fund is compared to the most stable on the list (T. Rowe Price Short-Term Bond). For example, the performance level increment for Vanguard Fixed-Income Short-Term Bond is found by subtracting $14,982 from $16,224. Performance instability increment for Vanguard is $541 − $328. The risk-adjusted performance index is the first difference above divided by the second difference.

The Vanguard index number, 5.83, means that each dollar cost

Table 6-2. Summary of Performance of Balanced, Growth, and Income Funds

Fund name	Average 3-year performance level	Performance instability	Risk-adjusted performance index
T. Rowe Price Short-Term Bond	$14,982	$ 328	—
Twentieth Century U.S. Government	15,190	537	0.99
Vanguard Fixed-Income Short-Term Bond	16,224	541	5.83
USAA Mutual Income	17,525	888	4.54
Permanent Portfolio	13,638	1,011	−1.96
Wellesley Income	19,772	1,300	4.93
Lindner	20,505	1,351	5.40
Stein-Roe Total Return	17,676	1,423	2.46
Mathers	21,872	1,497	5.90
Dodge and Cox Balanced	21,111	1,521	5.13
Burnham	21,311	1,551	5.17
Wellington	20,658	1,609	4.43
Lindner Dividend	19,304	1,612	3.37
Strong Investment	17,524	1,770	1.76
Fidelity Puritan	20,597	1,935	3.49
Nicholas	19,330	1,961	2.66
Eaton Vance Income-Boston	18,243	2,080	1.86

of increased performance instability in comparison to the T. Rowe Price standard is rewarded by the benefit of a $5.83 increase in average performance level. By comparing performance indexes among all funds on the list, you can see which offer the "best buys" in terms of trading higher risk for higher performance. The same logic applies to Table 6-3, although the risk-adjusted performance index would be interpreted to mean costs and benefits in percentages instead of dollars.

Table 6-3. Summary of Performance of Tax Avoidance Municipal Bond Funds

Fund name	Average 3-year performance level	Perfor-mance instability	Risk-adjusted performance index
Vanguard Municipal Fund Short-Term	34.53%	0.88%	—
Merrill Lynch Municipal Limited Maturity	33.71	0.95	−11.71
Calvert Tax Free Reserve-Limited	38.98	1.72	5.30
T. Rowe Price Tax Free Short-Intermediate	35.91	1.86	1.41
USAA Tax Exempt Short-Term	37.95	2.32	2.38
Limited Term Municipal-National	48.56	2.77	7.42

How Can You Put Together a Fund Selection Process?

The performance summary tables can be applied to guide choices about funds in accordance with your personal needs and desires. For example, if your emphasis is very strongly on low risk, you may prefer to select from only the lowest three in performance instability for your portfolio. Among these three funds, Vanguard is a "best buy" in terms of the index and therefore an obvious choice. However, although you desire low risk you may also want higher levels of growth and income than the average performance of Vanguard above. In that case, you might want to include some additional choices from among funds which have high average performance levels and high risk-adjusted indexes. To consider both trends and summary performance data simultaneously, transcribe the performance data onto the charts, as shown in Figures 6-7 through 6-11. Check marks indicate the more likely choices from each grouping represented on the charts. Some likely choices would seem to include Mathers, Dodge and Cox Balanced, Wellesley Income, and Burnham.

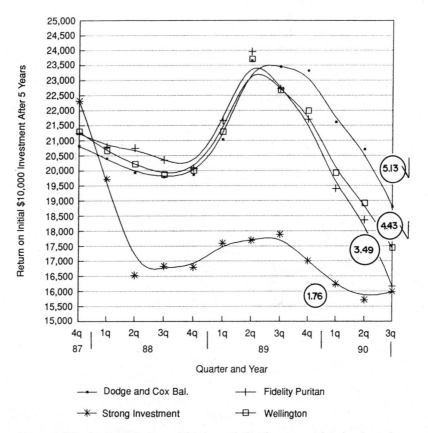

Figure 6-7. Low-risk balanced fund trends for 3 years, with risk-adjusted performance indexes.

About one-half of the funds listed would not be likely candidates for selection because of their lower index numbers. Similarly, in choosing among tax avoidance possibilities for a low-risk portfolio, Vanguard Municipal Bond Short-Term in the least risky, but Calvert provides a significant increment in average performance level in return for a small cost in terms of performance instability. If you wanted tax avoidance and higher performance levels for your portfolio, you might want to allocate a portion of your funds to the "riskier" Limited Term fund, because of the proportionately greater performance level increments you could hope to attain by tripling the performance instability associated with Vanguard Municipal Short-Term.

Ultimately, your choices depend on needs and preferences re-

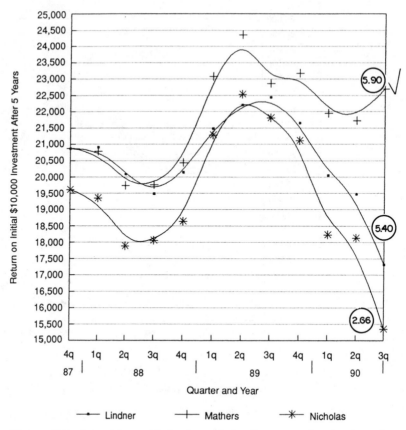

Figure 6-8. Low-risk growth fund trends for 3 years, with risk-adjusted performance index.

vealed earlier in your self-assessment and on your evaluation of contextual influences. As an example, recall that *Forbes* gives all the municipal bond fund possibilities very high ratings in down markets. If there were clear indications that the market would decline, these funds would have to be considered more favorably for at least some portion of your investments. It is also important to recognize that the distinction between growth and income as fund objectives is somewhat artificial, from the investors point of view. A growth fund can be a source of income through the redemption of shares, and an income fund can be a source of growth by reinvestment of returns. What is not artificial is performance level and stability.

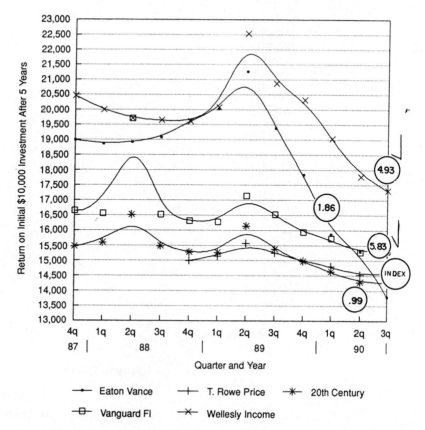

Figure 6-9. Low-risk income fund trends for 3 years, with risk-adjusted performance index.

Review of Portfolio Selection Process

1. Find sources of information that represent both current and recent historical ratings of mutual fund risk and performance.

2. Select for consideration from these sources the "best risks," "top performers," and "high-quality" mutual funds represented in these listings.

3. Portray graphically comparative performance trends for a recent period. (Make portfolio selections at this point if you do not want to conduct a numerical analysis, i.e., if you skipped the Summary of Performance section.)

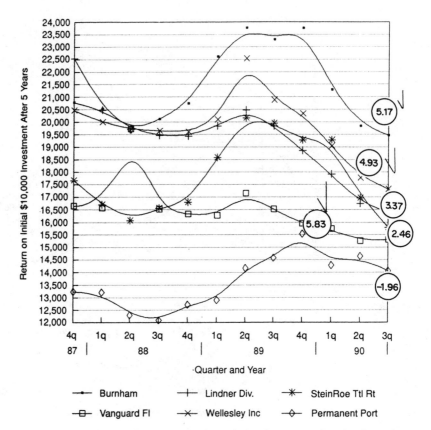

Figure 6-10. Low-risk income fund trends for 3 years, with risk-adjusted performance index.

4. Create performance summary tables which include average performance level, performance instability, and a risk-adjusted performance index.

5. Transcribe risk-adjusted performance index data onto the charts of performance trends.

6. Select funds for your portfolio based on your assessment of needs and preferences and on performance summary tables and charts. Look for best buys in terms of risk-adjusted performance index, and consider the direction and relationship of performance trends among funds as represented graphically. Avoid highly unstable funds, funds with low performance indexes, and funds which show performance trends decelerating more rapidly than peers.

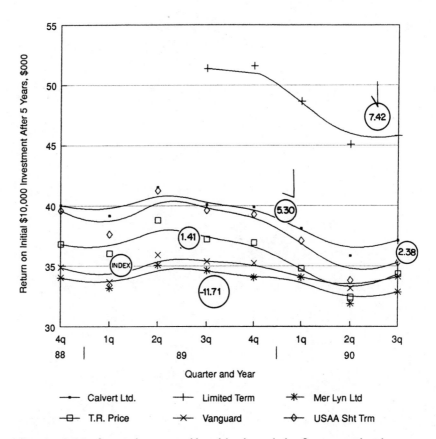

Figure 6-11. Low-risk municipal bond fund trends for 2 years, with risk-adjusted performance index.

7

High-Growth
Portfolios

In Chapter 7 you will assess three growth strategies:

1. *Current high-performance strategy.* Continually readjust your portfolio to reflect the most current listings of best-performing growth funds.

2. *Price-earnings ratio and interest rate strategy.* Trade in and out of stock and bond markets, using levels of P-E ratios and interest rates to guide your decisions.

3. *Fixed percentage allocation strategy.* Allocate a fixed percentage of your portfolio to certain growth sectors. As the percentage of assets changes as a result of differences in growth rates among these sectors, reallocate funds from the more highly successful sectors to achieve the original percentages once again.

You will see how well each of these strategies would have worked in recent years. Then, the methods of Chapter 6 will be applied to demonstrate how you could select the best choices among an array of growth funds. Finally, a summary reviews exactly what steps you need to take to make effective decisions in selecting a high-growth portfolio.

Current High-Performance Strategy

An article in *Business Week* offers the following brief description of the general approach:

> The strategy simply involves investing in a fund or small group of stock funds that performed best in the recent past. Then investors would periodically assess the performance of all similar funds and switch to the most recent winners.[1]

The article reports that the economists who developed this strategy examined how well it would have worked on 96 no-load growth funds from 1974 to 1987. Investors who switched funds each year into the five top performers would have achieved returns 5 to 10 percent higher than the S&P index. Switching every quarter or 6 months also paid off in their analysis, but holding the same group for more than 1 year didn't pay.

In this section you will use a performance measure that is more sensitive to short-term changes in mutual fund values than the 5-year total return on an initial $10,000 investment which we used in the last chapter. To test the hypothesis that periodic fund switching would have had utility in recent years, we are obliged to consider a short-term period that extends forward from the year of termination of the cited study to the present, i.e., 1988 to 1990. Since this period covers 12 quarters, it will be possible to see if the fund-switching strategy suggested above would have produced useful results if implemented on a quarterly level. Therefore, the performance measure would necessarily be the quarterly return on an initial $10,000 investment.

In order to see if fund switching is useful, some consistent basis for choosing the best performing funds needs to be devised. For the examples that follow, choices were made for four different portfolios of the five best-performing mutual funds, which carried no load or redemption fees, among those listed by *Barron's* in each of the following categories:

Best quarterly performance (not available in 1988)

Best 1-year performance

Best 5-year performance

Best 10-year performance

Table 7-1 provides average returns quarterly, and 2-year and 3-year total returns, for each category, based on an initial $10,000 investment. As you can see from the last lines of Table 7-1 quarterly fund switching yields its best results when you use the best 5-year or best 10-year performance lists. The results for the best-in-quarter list are dismal, showing a 9 percent net loss over 2 years. If you examine the mutual funds chosen from this list, you will find precious metal and international currency funds well represented. Variation in the values of precious metals and currencies account for both the high performance which made these funds eligible for best in quarter and the low performance they demonstrate after they are selected for the portfolio. Over the longer term, these variations cancel each other, and investment funds therefore dominate the longer-term lists.

Table 7-1. Average Portfolio Return Using Quarterly Fund Switching

Quarter	Best in quarter	Best in 1 year	Best in 5 years	Best in 10 years
1st Q/1988	NA	10,525	10,993	10,967
2nd Q/1988	NA	9,851	10,093	10,593
3rd Q/1988	NA	9,860	9,839	9,870
4th Q/1988	NA	10,748	11,025	10,229
1st Q/1989	10,594	11,322	10,205	10,743
2nd Q/1989	11,014	10,948	10,040	10,740
3rd Q/1989	10,189	11,400	11,793	11,172
4th Q/1989	10,000	9,989	10,279	10,097
1st Q/1990	9,229	9,714	9,225	9,514
2nd Q/1990	11,149	11,324	11,033	11,116
3rd Q/1990	7,777	7,251	8,523	8,321
4th Q/1990	9,547	10,191	10,929	10,536
Total 12Q	NA	12,393	14,172	13,720
Total 8Q	9,083	11,474	11,775	12,067

Table 7-2. Average Portfolio Return Using Annual Fund Switching

Year	Best in quarter	Best in 1 year	Best in 5 years	Best in 10 years
1988	NA	10,503	11,881	11,423
1989	13,195	14,106	12,262	12,327
1990	7,691	9,532	8,818	9,293
1988–1990 Total 3 year	NA	14,122	12,846	13,086
1989–1990 Total 2 year	10,148	13,446	10,813	11,455

What would have happened if we used annual fund shifting over this period? The results are shown in Table 7-2.

Here too, choosing from the best-in-quarter list is the worst strategy. However, the best 1-year list does much better in an annual switching approach and yields credible results over the 3-year period under consideration. Overall, quarterly switching does not appear more efficacious than annual.

If you compare these results to increasing values of the Standard and Poor's industrial index, you will find they are not as high, although they do exceed increases in the Dow Jones Industrial Index between 1987 and 1990.

Price-Earnings Ratios and Interest Rate Strategy

Would you have been able to forecast the tremendous increase in stock prices that took place during the 1980s and the October 1987 crash with publicly available and uncomplicated information? The answer is, from a practical point of view, you could have known when to shift funds into and out of the stock market in order to benefit from the price increase and avoid the sudden downturn that took 20 percent out of investors' pockets in 1 day. Here's how.

Figure 7-1 plots interest rates on 30-year treasuries on the *Y* axis

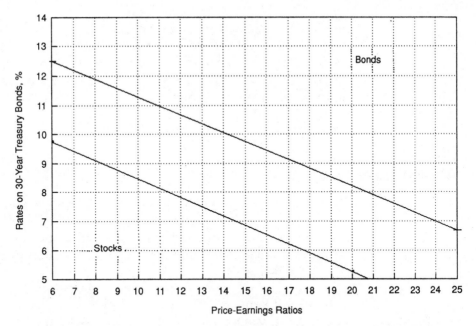

Figure 7-1. Guide to shifting assets between stocks and bonds based on price-earnings ratios and interest. (*Based on a chart prepared by Wright Investors Services,* Fortune, *Dec. 4, 1989, p. 52. Used with permission.*)

against the Standard and Poor's 500 index price-earnings ratios on the X axis. (Price-earnings ratios are stock prices divided by earnings. A high ratio means stocks are selling at a relatively high price, whereas a low number means they may be undervalued.) This information is regularly published in the personal investing section of *Fortune* magazine, in *Forbes,* and in other sources. The area above the two diagonals is labeled "bonds." Below the diagonals the area is labeled "stocks," and between two diagonals there is a blank area which can be called "zone of indecision." The graph proposes that very high interest rates or P-E ratios indicate a switch from stocks to bonds. Low interest rates and low P-E ratios favor moving from bonds to stocks. When interest rates and P-E ratios are at intermediate levels, it is not possible to clearly discern the best course of action.

During most recent years you would find that interest rates and P-E ratios for the S&P 500 would fall in the zone of indecision. However, during the early 1980s the graph would have correctly steered your investments into equities, whereas the subsequent increase in stock prices (which raised P-E ratios) would have helped you decide to switch to bonds prior to the October 1987 stock market crash. So, the strategy suggested by the graph would be useful for long-term decision making even if it contributes little to the short-term management of your investment account.

Fixed Percentage Allocation Strategy

To evaluate this strategy you need to choose a portfolio of funds from various growth sectors. From *Barron's* 2/15/88 list of top performers by investment objective, we find the following representative no-load funds and associated investment growth categories in the 5-year list:

Strong Total Return   Growth and income
Vanguard Hi Yield Stock   Equity income
T. Rowe Price New Era   Natural resources

   The 10-year list includes:

Twentieth Century Growth   Capital appreciation
Lindner Dividend   Equity Income

   Assume that 20 percent of your assets were allocated to each fund. For a $10,000 initial investment the scorecard after 1 year (1989) would read:

Sector	Initial allocation, %	Value after 1 year	Value after 1-year reallocation
Growth and income	20	$ 2,311	$ 2,316
Capital appreciation	20	2,054	2,316
Natural resources	20	2,206	2,316
Equity income	40	5,008	4,632
Total		$11,579	$11,580

   The second column shows change in the value of the original allocation after 1 year. At this point we reallocate the total of the second column to again obtain our original percentages, as shown in the third column.

By the end of 1989, the scorecard would have read:

Sector	Initial allocation, %	Value after 2 years	Value after 2-year reallocation
Growth and Income	20	$ 2,377	$ 2,700
Capital appreciation	20	3,272	2,700
Natural resources	20	2,879	2,700
Equity income	40	4,974	5,400
Total		$13,502	$13,500

Once again, we adjust the amounts in the second column to obtain the original percentages, as shown in the third column.

Finally, in December 1990 your fortune would look like this:

Sector	Value after 3 years
Growth and income	$ 2,508
Capital appreciation	2,596
Natural resources	2,463
Equity income	4,427
Total	$11,994

This example retains the same funds in each of four areas throughout the 3-year period of observation. The results show that reallocating a percentage of your assets without changing funds is less rewarding than investing in the performance of the Standard and Poor's 500 during this time period.

How Would You Choose a High-Growth Portfolio?

The method for choosing a low-risk portfolio formulated in Chapter 6 may also be applied to choose high-growth mutual funds. In the following abbreviated example we will rely on *Consumer Reports'* May 1990 issue as our initial source of information, although other sources are available and the example could be expanded to include them. From an examination of the funds listed we find that there are a limited number of no-load mutual funds which exceeded the performance of the S&P 500 index over the past 5 years. Those stock funds which invest in domestic securities include the following:

IAI Regional

Dodge and Cox Stock

Scudder Capital Growth

Twentieth Century Growth

Twentieth Century Vista

Stein-Roe Special

Founders Growth

No-load international funds that outperformed the S&P 500 in the last 5 years included:

Japan Fund

Kleinwort Benson International Equity

Vanguard World International Growth

T. Rowe Price International Stock

Scudder International

Review the performance summary table and charts which compare performance trends among these mutual funds for the same 3-year period used to assess strategy performance in the preceding section of this chapter (see Table 7-3 and Figures 7-2 and 7-3).

Many of the names on the performance summary table (Table 7-3) also appear in other listings used to analyze growth fund performance in this chapter. All the international funds made consistent appearances on *Barron's* best performers lists, and Twentieth Century Growth was a consistent best performer among domestic funds.

Because international fund performance was radically different from U.S. fund performance, the two categories are charted separately. There was far less variability among domestic funds, and performance levels have most sharply declined for international funds.

Among domestic mutual funds drawn from the *Consumer Re-*

Table 7-3. Performance Summary Table

Fund name	Average performance level	Perfor- mance instability	Risk-adjusted performance index
Dodge & Cox Stock	23,155	2,598	—
Stein-Roe Special	21,791	3,116	−2.63
IAI Regional	23,493*	3,340	0.46
Twentieth Century Vista	21,072	3,820	−1.70
Scudder International	28,083	3,971	3.58
Founders Growth	19,770	4,034	−2.36
Scudder Capital Growth	22,084	4,205	−0.67
Twentieth Century Growth	21,190	4,362	−1.11
T. Rowe Price Int'l Stock	30,503**	4,369	4.15
Vanguard World Int'l Growth	31,639	5,072	3.43
Japan Fund	35,729	5,876	3.83
Kleinwort Benson Int'l Equity	31,591	6,413	2.21

*Best-buy domestic fund

**Best-buy international fund

ports listing (see Figure 7-2), IAI regional appears to offer stability and consistently higher levels of performance in recent quarters. Twentieth Century Growth also seems to show a developing trend in recent performance that exceeds its historical relationship to the trends shown by other domestic funds in the list. From among the international funds (see Figure 7-3), T. Rowe Price International appears to have had the greatest stability over time, primarily because it never achieved the very high past performance levels of other funds, although it is currently doing well in relation to them. You would have lost far less money if you had invested in T. Rowe Price International 3 years prior to the end of 1990 than you would have lost in other international funds.

The three choices drawn from *Consumer Reports* suggested by the preceding paragraph may also be supplemented by reviewing funds on current best performer lists. Finally, you should allocate

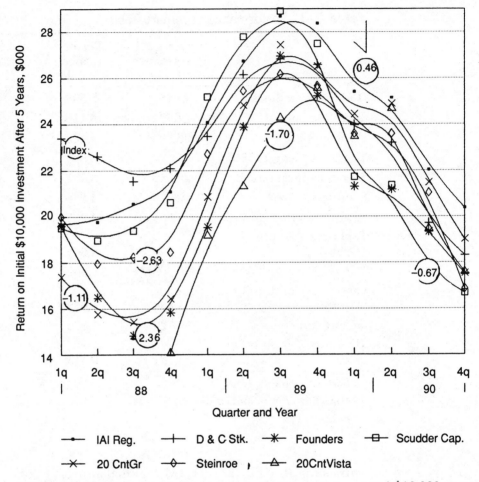

Figure 7-2. Domestic growth fund trends for 3 years (return on initial $10,000 investment after 5 years).

a portion of your funds to a well-managed S&P index fund, such as the Vanguard Index: 500 Portfolio.

Summary of High-Growth Fund Decision Steps

1. Examine lists of best-performing funds in *Barron's* and research which are best for annual, quarterly, or other duration reviews of your portfolio. You may or may not find that research in this area at the time you read this book will confirm

the use of 5-year best-performing lists for quarterly switching and 1-year lists for annual reviews, as suggested in this chapter. Do your own review and make up your own mind based on current information.

2. Look at P-E ratios and long-term interest rates to see if there is a clear indication that you should reallocate your investments from equities to debt securities, or vice versa.

3. Review other sources of expert opinion and lists of high-performing funds, such as the *Consumer Reports* example used

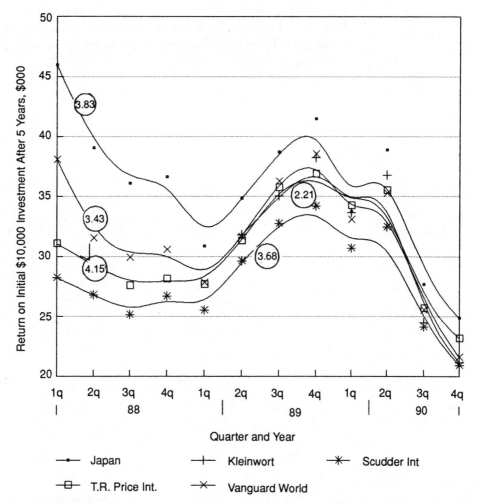

Figure 7-3. International fund trends for 3 years (return on initial $10,000 after 5 years).

earlier. Funds of different categories need to be included in this review (e.g., domestic versus international).

4. Select an array of funds and construct a performance summary table and/or graphs which portray recent trends.

5. Evaluate funds and select those which appear to be doing well relative to the entire array in recent periods. Consider all sources of information that you have included in your research in enlarging the range of possibilities. Be sure to select funds from more than one area, and include at least one index fund in your portfolio.

6. Remember, in making your selection, if you choose funds that lose less during a bear market you are also contributing to asset growth over the long-term, since you do not have to earn back the money lost.

8

High-Income Portfolios

This chapter will probably be of greatest interest to people who are retired or expecting to retire soon. To clarify the characteristics of the different types of mutual funds which produce income, we offer a survey of fixed-income securities and a number of alternatives in which these funds invest your money. The survey includes:

Treasury bonds, notes, and bills

Mortgage-backed securities

Other government agency bonds

Corporate bonds—investment quality

Corporate bonds—convertible to stock

Corporate bonds—high-yield (junk)

Preferred stock

Utilities stock

We will then review a number of important considerations in selecting a portfolio of income securities, such as:

1. Interest rate risk

2. Portfolio maturity

3. Investment quality

4. Management and sales fees

5. Yield to maturity

As in the past two chapters, we will select a portfolio of high-income mutual funds based on a review of fund performance in publicly available sources of information. Finally, a summary of the process for fund selection will be presented at the end of this chapter.

Survey of Fixed-Income Securities

Before you invest in a mutual fund which owns fixed-income securities, you need to know something about their characteristics.

Treasury Bonds, Notes, and Bills

U.S. Treasury securities are the safest of all investments. They are also liquid. Treasury bills are discounted at the time of sale and then paid at full face value at maturity, whereas notes and bonds are sold at par value and pay interest semiannually. On the secondary market, Treasury securities vary in price depending on current interest rates and time left to maturity, as do other debt securities. Interest paid is exempt from state and local taxes. Mutual funds that invest in U.S. government bond funds may differ in terms of their mix of maturities, either as a matter of fund policy and definition or because of portfolio management objectives that vary with changing market conditions. Only a very small proportion of U.S. families hold these securities independently of mutual funds, but they represent a substantial commitment of assets among the more affluent households.

Mortgage-Backed Securities

Three important U.S. government agencies purchase mortgage loans and then sell securities which pass through principal and interest payments to investors. Depending on their origin, these securities are called *Ginnie Maes* (GNMA—Government National Mortgage Association), *Fannie Maes* (FNMA—Federal National Mortgage Association), and *Freddie Macs* (FHLB—Federal Home

Loan Bank). These securities are collateralized by the houses on which mortgages are borrowed and are guaranteed by the government agencies that issue them. The major risks associated with these securities include decline of principal value in current markets if interest rates rise, and mortgage prepayments during periods when interest rates decline sharply. However, these securities typically yield higher interest than Treasury securities of comparable maturity. There are no tax exemptions on the interest paid, but a portion of the monthly payments received by investors is deemed to be return of principal, and no tax is paid on this part of the investor's income.

Fixed-income portfolio managers typically vary the proportion of assets allocated to mortgage-backed securities on the basis of anticipated change or stability of interest rate spreads between this and other types of securities, such as long-term Treasuries. An investor who wanted to actively manage mutual funds in a similar fashion could readily change asset allocation if the mutual funds were no loads but would pay significantly for the privilege if she or he invested in load funds.

Other Government Agency Bonds

In addition to mortgage-backed securities, the U.S. government issues bonds through various agencies such as the Small Business Administration, Student Loan Marketing Association, Export-Import Bank, Farmers Home Administration, and others. Bonds issued by these agencies have a wide range of maturity and are quite liquid and very secure except for interest rate risk. Their interest income is slightly higher than Treasuries and in most cases is exempt from state and local taxes.

Corporate Bonds— Investment Quality

Investment-quality corporate bonds have ratings from Moody's or Standard and Poor's which include no letters other than the letter "A." These are a favorite investment of insurance companies, which try to have a widely diversified portfolio and use them for two purposes. First, these bonds pay higher interest than U.S. government securities, and second, they can be matched quite readily to projected needs for cash arising out of anticipated liabilities. For example, (on an individual level) if you needed to pay for your child's first year college tuition in 2002, you might buy a high-grade corporate bond maturing in that year for an amount that matched what you expected to need in 2002. Although the value of your bond will vary with interest rates during the years intervening between dates of purchase and maturity, the corporation which issued the bond has pledged to pay the full face value in 2002. To the extent that the issuer is creditworthy, your investment is secure. Diversifying helps reduce risk of default, and mutual funds that invest in high-grade corporate bonds can accomplish this for you quite readily. There are even funds which specialize in bonds of a particular maturity should you prefer to target a particular period. But remember that the riskiness of the bond tends to increase as the time to maturity increases.

Corporate Bonds—Convertible to Stock

If you would be willing to take less in interest income from a corporate bond investment in order to have the opportunity to participate in the appreciation of the issuer's common stock, you may do so through the purchase of convertible bonds. This type of investment is somewhat more speculative than investment-grade corporate bonds that do not have the convertible privilege, but they also allow you to benefit from both declining interest rates and rising stock prices.

Corporate Bonds—High-Yield (Junk)

During the last half of the 1980s, junk bonds achieved both the zenith and nadir of their highly variable orbit in the financial sphere. Because they yield significantly more interest income than other investments, these bonds were highly attractive to institutions, including banks, pension funds, and some insurance companies, which accepted the theory that diversification of holdings could protect them against the risks associated with this highly speculative type of investment and that the higher interest the bonds paid would more than offset the greater possibility of default. Regrettably, vast sums were lost as the entire market for junk bonds collapsed, with far-reaching implications and losses reaching across the U.S. economy. One complaint of the premier junk bond brokerage house, the now defunct Drexel Burnham Lambert, was that the Federal Reserve Bank refused to intervene to provide liquidity in support of the junk bond market, as it had for the stock market during the 1987 crash. With this fact in mind, one may conclude that investment in stock may be less risky than investments in junk bonds for as long as the Fed sustains its policy. Do not buy junk bond mutual funds except as a complete speculation.

Preferred Stock

Although they represent equity in a company, preferred stocks resemble bonds in providing income through dividends that are a fixed percentage of their face value. Unlike interest paid on bonds, preferred stock dividends may be withheld during a given year without forcing the company into legal proceedings. However, unlike common stock dividends, if withheld, preferred dividends are often cumulative and remain obligations of the company until paid. Preferred stocks offer a slightly higher yield than corporate bonds and are price-sensitive to interest rate variations as are bonds. They are less secure than bonds but more secure than common stocks of the same issuer. Some preferred stocks are convertible to common stock. Convertible preferreds allow for appreciation in market value tied to the ascent of a company's common stock and provide protection against declines in stock price to the extent of their ability to produce a fixed income. However, if interest rates rise at the same time as the stock market declines, which is often the case, convertible preferred will offer no protection against declining values.

Utilities Stocks

Because of their heavy capital requirements and because of regulatory considerations, utilities are in almost constant need of debt financing. Utilities stocks, to some extent, represent a surrogate for debt. Because of this, and because of their relatively large dividend pay out, they are influenced by current interest rate conditions. When interest rates are low, utilities stocks can be attractive investments because of their stable earnings and security. When interest rates rise rapidly, these companies are not able to quickly adjust their fees to consumers because of the restrictions on rate increases imposed by regulatory authorities. As a result, profits can be threatened by interest rate volatility.

Fixed-Income Portfolio Risks and Considerations

Keep in mind a number of issues when you are choosing funds for a high-income portfolio (some of these have been alluded to in the discussion in the preceding section):

What Is Interest Rate Risk?

Although this issue has been discussed earlier, it is worth mentioning again in relation to this type of investment portfolio because it is so pervasive and strong an influence on both performance and choice of investments in this area. All long-term fixed-income investments are price-sensitive to changes in interest rates. Interest rates, in turn, incorporate both inflationary and market components that may not be highly predictable. Some convertible securities may offer partial protection against interest rate risk under certain circumstances, but the only truly effective hedge against interest rate risk is to maintain a portfolio which includes short-term and/or rotating maturities. With such an arrangement, a portion of your assets will be coming due in cash periodically, allowing for reinvestment at current rates. The drawback to such a strategy is that current rates may be lower as well as higher than those received in the past.

What Should You Know about Portfolio Maturity?

In general, the longer the term of average maturity of a bond fund portfolio, the higher the return and the greater the interest rate risk. Average maturity is a critical feature of any bond portfolio and needs to be considered when making choices and comparing bond fund performance. The value of a bond depends on the length of time remaining to maturity, as well as the current interest rates. Since the future is unpredictable, longer maturities tend to compound other risks associated with bond ownership, such as inflation and potential changes in asset quality as the fortunes of corporations and government entities wax and wane over time.

What Should You Know about Investment Quality?

During the onset of the 1990s, investment quality has become a far more important characteristic of the financial business than at any time since the Great Depression. A number of issues—the notorious failure of many large savings and loan institutions, and the thrift industry in general, because of the collapse of real estate and junk bond markets; the possibility of a similar disaster in banking; as well as the failure of certain insurance companies— have left an impression on public attitudes of concern for the safety and security of investments. During the 1980s, those financial organizations which took the greatest risks and gained the best returns were most admired. However, with the reversals experienced by these same organizations just a few years later, many of these organizations have failed or at least lost much in public esteem. However, conservatively managed firms have become much admired, whereas in the past their managements were derided as "sleepy" or "brain-dead." The lesson for the smaller investor is that risk actually counts for something and is not simply an abstract, meaningless concept. Quality in investments usually costs something, but poor quality may have ultimately a much higher cost in both lost interest and principal.

Management and Sales Fees

Barron's regularly prints an article which describes the effects of sales charges (loads) on returns. The method of computing postload returns is not difficult. First, subtract the load percentage from 100 percent (e.g., for a 2 percent load, subtract 2 percent from 100 percent). Express the remainder as a decimal (e.g., 0.980), then multiply times fund performance. For example, if the 5-year compound return of a given fund was $20,000, and the sales charges were 2 percent, than the postload return would be $19,600 ($20,000 × 0.980). Redemption fees, and the cumulative effect of management fees, also proportionately reduce your return. For this reason you should consider the total cost of owning a fund before you buy and carefully examine returns after fees are deducted if you are purchasing a load fund.

What Is Yield to Maturity?

A bond's current yield is its current annual interest payment divided by its current price. For example, a bond selling for $1000 and paying $80 per year in interest has an 8 percent current yield. But as interest rates change, the value of a bond fluctuates. The bond can be selling for more or less than its par value. Such bonds are purchased at a premium or a discount and decrease or increase in value as the maturity date nears, since they will be redeemed at face value at maturity. So, the yield (called the "yield to maturity") will be higher or lower than the current yield. You can compute the yield to maturity exactly with a financial calculator or financial tables, or yield to maturity may be calculated approximately using the following formula:

$$Y = \frac{(\text{current interest/payment}) + \dfrac{[(\$1000 - \text{current bond balance})/ \text{number of years to maturity}]}{}}{(\$1000 + \text{current bond price})/2}$$

If the bond is selling at face value, there is no difference between current yield and yield to maturity. When bonds are selling above or below face value, the above formula approximates the yield to maturity. The yield to maturity may be critical in planning the use of a bond to offset expected future liabilities or to meet financial goals, such as retirement fund principal on which to calculate projected retirement income.

How Do You Select a High-Income Portfolio?

In the February 11, 1991, issue of *Barron's* you can find among top performers of 1990 identified by investment category that there are four no-load funds without redemption fees which are characterized as income funds:

Wellesley Income

Wasatch Income

Unified Income

Dividend/Growth: Dividend

Changing Times (September 1990) identifies several top-performing no-load funds:

Growth and income	Vista Growth and Income
	Monetta (Growth and Income)
High-grade corporate	Scudder Short-Term Bond
	Newberger & Berman Ltd. Maturity
	Vanguard Fixed Income—Short Term
	Flex Bond
International	Scudder International Bond

In *Business Week* (2/18/91), top performers for income include the following no-load funds:

USAA Mutual Income

Wellesley Income

In the next week's issue, the best bond funds include the following no-loads on the list:

Delaware Treasury Reserves

Dreyfus Short-Intermediate Government

Federated Income (Government Mtg.)

Federated Short-Intermediate Government

IAI Reserve (Corporate)

Income Portfolios Short Government

Newberger Berman Ltd. Maturity (Corporate)

Permanent Portfolio Treasury Bills

T. Rowe Price Short-Term Bond

Scudder Short-Term Bond

Value Line U.S. Government Securities

Vanguard Fixed-Income Short-Term Bond

Vanguard Fixed-Income Short-Term Government

In *Consumer Reports* (June 1990) the following corporate bond no-load funds are listed as having high-quality portfolios:

Vanguard Fixed-Income Short-Term Bond

Vanguard Fixed-Income Investment Grade

Dreyfus A Bonds Plus

Scudder Income

Fidelity Flexible Bond

Fidelity Intermediate Bond

T. Rowe Price New Income

Government bond funds listed as no-loads include:

Vanguard Fixed-Income GNMA

Twentieth Century U.S. Government

Fidelity Mortgage Securities

Fidelity Government Securities

Pru-Bache Government Securities Intermediate

In total, our listing of possible no-load income funds amounts to 38 entries, including some repeated names. Since we could proceed further by reviewing other resources, this listing could be increased significantly. However, the effort required to review and chart performance for all these funds is beyond our capacity or desire. What is necessary is to devise one or more decision rules we can use to select a smaller array from among these initial, first-stage candidates. You, of course, are at liberty to think of whatever criteria make sense to you as a basis for reducing the size of the list. For example, one criterion might be to select funds in which you have some special interest for any reason. You might be interested in examining the performance of funds on the list that belong to well-known fund families. If this were the case you could choose the following array:

Scudder Short-Term Bond

Scudder International Bond

Scudder Income

Vanguard Fixed-Income Short-Term Bond

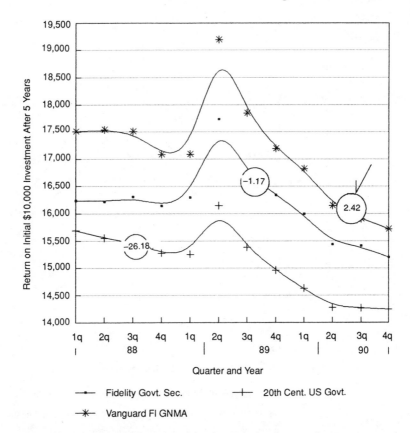

Figure 8-1. Government bond fund trends for 3 years (return on initial $10,000 investment after 5 years). See page 163.

Vanguard Fixed-Income Short-Term Government

Vanguard Fixed-Income Investment Grade

Vanguard Fixed-Income GNMA

T. Rowe Price Short-Term Bond

T. Rowe Price New Income

Twentieth Century U.S. Government

Fidelity Flexible Bond

Fidelity Intermediate Bond

Fidelity Mortgage Securities

Fidelity Government Securities

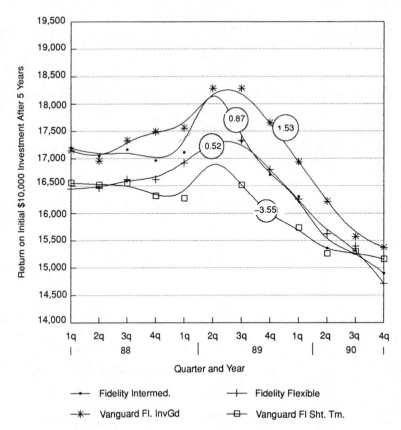

Figure 8-2. Selected corporate bond fund trends for 3 years (return on initial $10,000 investment after 5 years).

Another decision rule might be to select funds which have appeared as superior performers in other analyses we have conducted, such as those presented in earlier chapters of this book. This rule would add the following additional choices to our array:

Wellesley Income

Vista Growth and Income

USAA Mutual Income

IAI Reserve

With this reduced list of 18 funds it is possible to proceed with chart and table construction in order to compare performances. The funds should be grouped into corporate and government

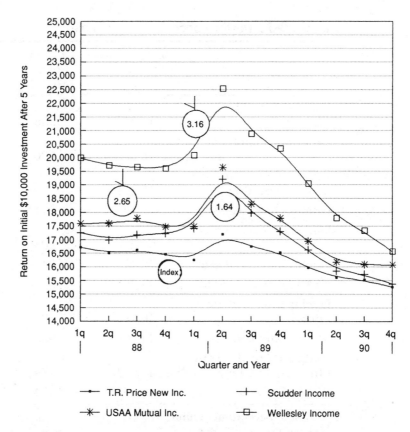

Figure 8-3. Selected corporate bond fund trends for 3 years (return on initial $10,000 investment after 5 years).

groupings when we conduct our comparisons. Results are shown in Figures 8-1 to 8-3 and Table 8-1 for 11 of the 18 funds for which complete information was available. From the table and figures it is apparent that you would be inclined to choose 3 of the 11 funds based on a 3-year performance review:

Vanguard Fixed-Income GNMA

USAA Mutual Income

Wellesley Income

These funds yielded the highest returns and appear to have the best risk-adjusted performance of all funds in this array. Choices

Table 8-1. Performance Summary Table

Fund	Average 3-year performance level	Perfor-mance instability	Risk-adjusted performance index
T. Rowe Price New Income	16,275	555	—
Twentieth Century-U.S. Govt.	15,097	596	−26.18
Vanguard Fixed-Income Short-Term Bond	16,101	600	−3.55
Fidelity Govt. Securities	16,169	641	−1.17
Vanguard Fixed-Income GNMA	17,129*	904	2.42
Fidelity Flexible Bond	16,481	944	0.52
USAA Mutual Income	17,400**	976	2.65
Fidelity Intermediate Bond	16,663	998	0.87
Scudder Income	17,006	998	1.64
Vanguard Fixed-Income Investment Grade	17,203	1,159	1.53
Wellesley Income	19,447**	1,554	3.16

*Best buy government fund
**Best buy corporate fund

made here could also be supplemented by low-risk income fund choices considered in Chapter 6.

Summary of High-Income Fund Decision Steps

1. Decide on the kinds of income funds you want to invest in based on a consideration of the types of securities they own and manage.

2. Review your decision about types of funds in terms of the fixed-income portfolio risks and considerations presented in this chapter:

Interest rate risk
Portfolio maturity
Investment quality
Management and sales fees
Yield

3. Consult the various resources and advisory publications which are pertinent to the fund types you have chosen. Select an array of funds that represent high performers among these fund types.

4. Construct performance summary charts and/or tables. Review comparative fund performance.

5. Select for your portfolio best buys which represent the fund types you want to include. Supplement your selection with choices from low-risk income groupings in order to achieve the balance of risk and yield you desire.

9

High Tax Avoidance Portfolios

This chapter begins with some general advice and then a discussion of tax avoidance vehicles which operate to defer taxes and thereby maximize capital accumulation through mutual fund ownership. Two of these, variable annuities and variable life contracts, are insurance company products. Two others, individual retirement accounts and Keogh plans are offered by a variety of financial institutions. The last of these, 401(k) plans, are uniquely offered through employers as supplementary pension plans. After this section, you will read about using municipal bonds and municipal bond funds to achieve tax-exempt investment income. Then we will work through an example of selecting the portfolio of municipal bond funds. Finally, the decision process will be summarized at the chapter's end to provide a brief reminder of the steps to take in selection of a high tax avoidance portfolio.

Keep Your Perspective

Many years ago a prominent judge wrote in a tax ruling that no citizen should feel obligated to pay more income tax than the minimum that the law required. Tax avoidance can be a legitimate aim of investing, and some types of investment maximize the potential saving on taxes.

Tax avoidance may be accomplished in ways that are unrelated to investment strategy. For example, you can take advantage of home mortgage and home equity loan interest deductions, you may find lawful ways of deferring income and gains, or you may use averaging techniques as allowed by the Internal Revenue Service. When you decide to follow an investment strategy which optimizes tax avoidance, it is of paramount importance that you not lose your perspective by focusing too narrowly on the tax avoidance issue. Always keep in mind that tax considerations are only one of the many factors that affect your investments' return and quality. Remember, there are ways to avoid paying taxes, including getting too low a return on your investment or suffering real losses of principal, that are more undesirable than paying taxes. Furthermore, the purpose of an investment should be primarily to make a good return, not to escape taxation. If it also helps to reduce your taxable income below what it would be in another good investment, so much the better. But do not lose sight of the goal of investing. So, you need to keep in mind both the investment and personal context in which you are pursuing tax avoidance objectives.

One example of what may happen if you lose your perspective was provided by a news article which reported on a lawsuit brought by unhappy investors against a Florida school district. The suit alleges that a representative of a major brokerage firm taught a course on investing in which the plaintiffs enrolled. As a result of their participation, these investors developed a client relationship with the teacher who sold them tax-advantaged limited partnerships, for which he earned high commissions. However, the investments fared poorly and were highly illiquid. As a result, the plaintiffs were left holding investments that produced no income, which they could not sell. Since the investments they made represented their life savings for retirement, these investors were ill-advised to have sought tax advantages above their most important goals of safety and stable income.

Tax Reform

Prior to the tax reform act of 1986 there were many vehicles for tax avoidance that either no longer exist or are far less important now than they were. Some examples are the special treatment afforded capital gains, depreciation allowances on income-producing real estate, oil and gas limited partnerships, and consumer loan interest rate deductions.

In return for the closing of these loopholes in the tax law, citizens were granted reductions in the tax rate. As a consequence of this change, tax avoidance is both less readily available than in the past and a less prominent investment feature than it was when rates were much higher.

Marginal Tax Rate

Although it is public knowledge which tax rates apply at given income levels, it is important to distinguish between these average tax rates and the marginal tax rates as they apply to your situation. The marginal rate is the rate you would pay on an additional dollar that you earned. For example, if you had an income of $50,000 and you earned an additional dollar which was taxed at 28 percent, your marginal rate of taxation is 28 percent. But your overall rate (or average) allowing for various deductions and exemptions would probably be much lower. For example, if you are paying high interest on a home mortgage, have largely tax-exempt or deferred investments, and earn a relatively low salary, it is entirely possible that the marginal tax you might have to pay on each dollar of additional income is as low as 15 percent. Therefore, if you had money to invest, it would probably be more to your advantage to seek a high rate of return in place of tax exemptions coupled to a lower yield. To find your own marginal rate look at your last tax return and calculate how much more tax you would have paid if you had earned an additional $100.

When is tax avoidance important? Tax avoidance matters most when your income is high and you would sacrifice a substantial proportion of investment income and gains to the tax collectors. It is also a critical feature of capital accumulation plans to at least defer tax payments to a future time when non-investment income may be lower. The reason for this is that even a small difference in investment return will ultimately result in a large difference in capital accumulation through compounding over time.

Variable Annuities and
Variable Life Insurance

At this point you may want to consider two other possible types of investment products. The two types of investments considered here should be considered long-term investments. Furthermore, you should carefully investigate the fees before buying, because fees vary widely and can be rather large. The tax-advantaged status of such plans may offset the impact of fees if you intend to stay with the investment for a long enough time, but this is something you should carefully consider before you invest. These products have some of the properties of mutual funds and some of the properties of annuities or life insurance products. They are not for everyone, but if tax avoidance is an important goal for you, or if your insurance needs are not fully satisfied, you should consider whether one or both of these products should be in your portfolio. The income tax law changes during the 1980s eliminated many tax shelters, while lowering the tax rates. But life insurance products escaped efforts to curtail their tax-advantaged status and so continue to enjoy certain tax advantages.

Traditional (fixed) life insurance and fixed annuity contracts have a definite "cash value"—the amount of money you would get if you returned the contract to the company and asked for a lump sum payment in the amount of its current value—which grows in accordance with the terms of the contract. Generally, a minimum rate of interest is specified as is an estimated or projected or illustrative rate the company plans to pay. The insurance company will supply a copy of a spreadsheet which shows the growth in cash value (how much the contract will be worth if it is cashed in) after various periods of time (1 year, 2 years, 3 years, etc.) based on these rates. This growth in the cash value of the contract is often referred to as the "inside buildup" of an annuity or insurance contract. This inside buildup escaped attempts to tax it during the battles of the 1980s.

Variable annuities and variable life insurance are designed by actuaries on principles used for all life insurance products, and they are issued by life insurance companies. These investments participate in these tax advantages enjoyed by life insurance products but also have some of the characteristics of mutual funds.

Unlike fixed-value insurance and annuity products, variable life insurance and variable annuities have cash values that cannot be spelled out in advance but vary according to the performance of the investment portfolio on which the product is based. The values can go up or down in response to the performance of the underlying investment portfolio. In this respect these products resemble mutual funds, but variable annuities and variable life insurance also have some similarities to their insurance cousins.

Variable Life Insurance

If you need additional life insurance protection to cover a mortgage or provide for income for dependents in the event of your death, you might want to consider variable life insurance. Like annuities, variable life insurance should be considered a long-term investment. If you need temporary life insurance coverage (for a car loan) for example you might be better off buying term insurance for the specified period. Like variable annuities, variable life insurance was designed to hedge against the ravages of inflation. An ordinary cash value life insurance policy that was adequate when purchased may become inadequate as the years go by as inflation eats away at its value. Just ask someone who bought a $10,000 policy several decades ago when $10,000 seemed like a great deal of life insurance.

Variable life policies have a minimum death benefit, but the death benefit and the cash value can grow based on the performance of the investments that underlie the policy. Like ordinary whole life insurance, the premium for a variable life insurance policy is fixed, and the policy contains a provision for borrowing against the cash value at a specified interest rate (often around 8 percent). Unlike ordinary whole life insurance, there is no minimum rate of return on your cash value—the rate depends on how well the investments for the variable life policies perform.

Variable life, like other insurance and annuity plans, retains the tax-deferred buildup feature (previously explained) that is applicable to life insurance contracts. If you need to withdraw money from your variable life policy, a policy loan can readily by arranged by contacting the insurance company. You should, of course, check with the life insurance company for the details of the policy loan provision.

Annuity Basics

Before considering variable annuities, we should briefly review some principles of annuities in general. The word *annuity* comes from the Latin word for year. The implication is that an annuity is a payment that you receive each year, though in actuality, annuity payments are usually made monthly. In a sense, an annuity is the reverse of a life insurance policy. A life insurance policy insures you against the risk that you will die too soon, i.e., before you can accumulate a large enough estate (assets) to pay off your debts and take care of your dependents' needs. Annuities insure against the risk that you will live too long, i.e., that your money will run out before you die.

With life insurance you pay a small premium to get a guarantee from the insurance company that a much larger payment will be made to your beneficiary in the event of your death. An annuity, by contrast, pays regular payments consisting of principal and interest to you for life, after you have paid the insurance company a relatively large payment. You are, in effect, buying a stream of income payments. Obviously, an important consideration in buying such a stream of payments is the rate of interest the company will pay on your money, since this will largely determine the amount of each payment you will receive from the annuity issuer. Other considerations include the safety of the company issuing the annuity, its proficiency in managing money, and its efficiency (low overhead) in running its operations—this will determine how much of your money will actually go toward providing you with annuity payments as opposed to paying company expenses, salaries, fees, or commissions.

Although a high rate of interest is desirable for the customer, the annuity company must be careful not to commit itself to making annuity payments to its customers that are higher than it can reasonably afford to pay. In other words, the company must be able to earn enough money on the money it has received to generate the payments it has promised to make to its customers and pay its own expenses and earn a reasonable profit. So the insurance company's management wants to offer high enough rates to attract prospective customers and get what it considers a sufficient amount of money from annuity sales. But a company that makes the mistake of setting its rates too high may find it has committed itself to making payments it will not be able to afford. This is why annuity companies sometimes get into financial trouble. To make things worse, annuity payments may extend many years, so a small error now can become a major error over the years of payments the company has contracted to make.

Several large insurance companies had this sort of problem with annuity or other investment products in the late 1980s and early 1990s. These problems usually occurred either because they set their rates too high or because they invested in risky investments that failed to pay off as they had hoped—leaving the insurance company unable to meet its commitments. In addition, when the policyholders or annuity holders begin to sense trouble, they may begin to try to get their money out rather like the way that the depositors demanded their money back from Jimmy Stewart in the classic movie *It's a Wonderful Life*.

Customers should therefore be careful when buying annuities to restrict their purchases to very strong insurance companies. Several organizations rate the strength of insurers, including Standard and Poor's, Moody's, and A.M. Best. *Money* magazine (July 1991), listed the strongest life insurance companies (ranked by assets) as follows:

Prudential

Metropolitan

New York Life

Connecticut General

John Hancock

Northwestern Mutual

Principal Mutual

Massachusetts Mutual

Nationwide

State Farm Life

Guardian Life

Since companies' financial conditions change over time, you should check on their current financial strength before doing business with them.

Origin of Annuities

Annuities originated to satisfy a need. Often people faced the problem of having accumulated a nest egg that they would now have to live on for the rest of their lives. Generally, this happened with people nearing retirement who had accumulated assets for retirement or with people who had suffered a disabling injury and been awarded a sum of money from a court settlement. Faced with the problem of how to use the assets to maximize their enjoyment of their retirement years (or ease their financial burdens) during their remaining years of life, they had a difficult problem. Since they could not know exactly how long they would live, they had no way of knowing exactly how much to spend. For the super rich this is not much of a problem, since no matter how much they spend, and for how long, there will be plenty more left. The very poor will not have enough, no matter what they do. The successful, hard-working people who face this situation have a difficult decision. If they knew precisely how long they would live, they would spend the right combination of earnings and principal to maximize their income and have the assets totally depleted on the day they died. In other words, they wanted to use the principal, and the earnings on the principal, so that they would have the maximum amount of money to spend but would not run out of money before they died. This turned out to be an ideal problem for life insurance companies to tackle. They have investment departments to try and get the maximum investment return on the annuity customers' money and actuaries who compile statistics on how long people live (on average) and experience with contracts that may require payments many years in the future. So life insurance companies have the required resources to issue annuities.

Today, a person who plans to retire can turn over assets to an insurance company and get a guaranteed income for life and not have to worry about spending the money too fast and ending penniless or spending it too slowly and not being able to enjoy retirement only to have assets passed on to (possibly) ungrateful relatives or eaten away by taxes or legal fees at death.

Types of Annuity Contracts

There are many variations and complications in annuity contracts, but the simplest type of annuity consists of the customer paying a lump sum to the insurance company at the time the payments are to begin (often at age 65) and receiving a guarantee of a check, for a specified amount, each month for the remainder of the customer's life. This is called an "immediate, straight-life annuity." It is immediate because the payments are scheduled to begin immediately, not at some specified time in the future. It is a straight-life annuity because the payments continue for the duration of the customer's life and then stop. The customer could get one check and then die, in which case the payments would stop after a single check, and the company would keep the remainder of the money. Alternatively, if the customer continues to live to a very old age (let us say 115), the insurance company must continue to make the stipulated monthly payment.

Many annuity customers do not want annuities that could result in their giving the life insurance company a large amount of money and getting only a single payment or a few payments if the customer should die soon after the payments begin. Furthermore, many annuity customers are married or have dependents or reasons to include other people in the payments. A husband may want an annuity that continues payments to himself or his wife as long as either is alive. An annuity contract may specify that the payments will continue to a beneficiary for a certain time or until the original amount deposited with the company has been paid out in monthly payments.

Instead of making a single premium payment to the insurance company, the annuity buyer may build up the asset value of the annuity over many years by making monthly payments into the plan and getting payments which start at retirement or on some other date many years in the future. There are many variations and complications of the basic annuity idea, so annuity contracts can be quite complex, but the underlying idea is (at least in principle) rather simple. In addition to using annuities to pay out the customer's assets the remainder of his or her life, they have come to be used as investment vehicles or as ways of paying out prizes (lottery winnings) or court judgments (structured settlements). The advantage of such uses is that the insurance company does the administrative work of keeping the records, making out the checks, and investing the principal, and the buyer of the annuity can go back to the normal business of selling lottery tickets or practicing law. Also the lottery commission can claim a higher prize than they actually have to pay out. For example, they could advertise a $20 million lottery prize by paying $1 million per year to the winner, whereas after putting the amount out for bids to competing insurance companies, the lottery commission will only pay a fraction of $20 million to settle with the winner.

Annuities sold for investment reasons are often single premium, which means that the customer pays the insurance company a single payment and the company invests the money for a number of years before paying the accumulated proceeds back to the customer whether in annuity payments or in a lump sum. A popular investment annuity is called the SPDA, or single-premium deferred annuity.

Variable Annuities

So far we have been talking about fixed annuities where the amounts involved are specified and the earnings on the invested amounts are known when the contract is signed. An alternative type of annuity is the variable annuity. In a variable annuity, the customer's rate of return on the investment is not known in advance. It depends on how well the investments chosen by the investment managers perform.

Variable annuities arose because in times of high inflation the earning on fixed investments such as fixed annuities are eroded by inflation. The variable annuity may enable the investor to offset some of or all the effects of inflation—since inflation may push up the value of the annuity portfolio's assets as well or the portfolio manager may choose rapidly appreciating assets—while still having many of the other advantages of an annuity. Of course, the variable annuity owner gives up the certainty associated with the fixed values of a fixed annuity. There is no guaranteed minimum rate of return with a variable annuity. Rather, the customer (also called the "annuitant") selects from a variety of types of investments managed by the insurance company. The annuitant usually has the option to switch among the various types of investments available under the plan, subject to some limitations.

The earnings on annuities are tax-sheltered until withdrawals begin, but there are penalties for withdrawing prematurely. Generally, you can remove up to 10 percent of the principal that has been in the annuity for more than 1 year without penalty. If you exceed 10 percent, you face a 5 percent penalty. After 7 years, any amount of principal can be withdrawn without charge. There may also be tax penalties on early withdrawals. Check with the insurance company and your tax advisor for details of the contract provisions and applicable tax rules.

As with fixed annuities, there is generally a provision for borrowing against the cash value of your annuity. If you name a beneficiary, in the event of your death your beneficiary will receive the death benefit as with any insurance policy. Check with the insurance company for the details about the death benefit, but generally it provides that the beneficiary will receive at least as much as you deposited (less any withdrawals you have made) or the current cash value of the annuity.

The annuities discussed above are nonqualified annuities, meaning that they are not given special tax treatment as are IRA plans, Keogh plans, or 401(k) plans. Qualified annuities purchased under such plans receive additional tax advantages as applicable to those plans.

If you decide to include variable annuities or variable life insurance in your investment portfolio, you should use the same process described previously for selecting funds. The performance numbers can be obtained from the statistical pages in *Barron's*. After you buy, you can check on how well your variable annuity or variable life policy investments are doing by looking in *Barron's* each week for the section that gives quotes on these contracts. Alternatively, you could ask the insurance company for the quotes.

Individual Retirement Accounts (IRAs)

Under current tax law you may claim deductions from current income for your contributions to an IRA, in full, if your adjusted gross income is less than $40,000 (for a married couple filing jointly). Partial deductions are allowed for joint income up to $50,000.

Even if you earn too much income to benefit from the deductibility feature, there are still advantages to contributing up to the maximum of $2000 annually to an IRA. Because of the deferral of taxation until funds are withdrawn, all investment earnings are compounded in full over the years, resulting in much larger accumulations. Over a 30-year period, the resulting sum in a mutual fund invested in an IRA account will greatly exceed that of a fully taxable mutual fund, even at the same rate of growth and especially if tax rates are high.

Withdrawal of funds without penalty may begin at age 59½, and the withdrawal becomes mandatory at age 70½. No contributions may be made after this age is reached. Withdrawn funds are taxed as ordinary income.

IRAs may be used to "roll over" funds from other pension plans in order to avoid tax penalties imposed on early withdrawal from such plans. For example, if you changed employers and could not transfer tax-deferred assets from your pension plan to a new employer, these could be placed in an IRA and no tax penalty would accrue.

In recent years many IRA owners have shifted their IRAs from banks to mutual funds because of declining short-term interest rates on bank deposits.

Keogh Accounts

Keogh accounts are primarily used by affluent self-employed persons, although most people who fit this description do not take advantage of this tax-deferral plan. A Keogh account is a pension plan for self-employed business owners. The plan has significant tax advantages, to a greater degree than IRAs. It permits deductions from current income of up to $30,000 (25 percent of compensation) for plan contributions. As in the case of IRAs, investment gains are tax deferred, and the plan may invest its assets in mutual funds. You may own both a Keogh and an IRA. However, eligibility requirements for Keogh plans include these conditions—self-employment, the business is not incorporated, and you are filing for self-employment social security taxes.

401(k) Plans

If you are not self-employed, you may be able to make use of a tax-deferred pension capital accumulation plan in addition to your IRA. A 401(k) plan is designed to offer employees the opportunity to make their own deductible contributions and to permit matching funds to be added by the employer. Requirements for withdrawal without penalty are the same as for an IRA. Although employees may contribute up to 25 percent of salary or $30,000, $7000 of this contribution may be deducted from current income. Investment gains are tax-deferred. A majority of large U.S. corporations now offer 401(k) plans to employees. Many employers provide mutual fund options to employees for investment of 401(k) assets.

Municipal Bonds

Although interest paid on municipal bonds is not currently taxed, it may be in the future. The advantage of this tax exemption depends on the investor's marginal tax rate. To calculate an equivalent taxable yield, simply subtract your marginal tax rate (discussed earlier in this chapter) from 1.00, then divide this result into the tax-exempt yield. For example, if a municipal bond pays 6.0 percent interest and is exempt from federal income taxes, then you could calculate an equivalent taxable yield as follows:

1. Subtract marginal tax rate from 1.00 (for example, deduct 0.15 from 1.00, equal to 0.85).
2. Divide 6.00 by 0.85, equal to 7.06.

For municipal bonds in your own state, which are also exempt from state and local taxes, you need only include these in computing a marginal tax rate to apply the above method of calculation. Obviously, the greater your marginal tax rate, the more advantageous the tax exemption option becomes. Federal bonds are exempt from state and local taxes, and this might influence your choice of investments if you live in a location where these taxes are high, such as New York City.

What Are the Sources of Risk for Municipal Bonds?

Municipal bonds are subject to the same kinds of risk as are other debt securities. Market prices will fall as interest rates rise. State and local governments and other issuers of municipal bonds have been known to default on interest and principal, and rating agencies review and rate many such bonds. However, changes in creditworthiness may also adversely affect market price. There may also be some difficulty in maintaining bond liquidity for small municipalities.

Some insurance companies insure municipal bonds against default. These insured bonds usually get high ratings from investment rating services and offer lower yields. Most of the insurers which issue such guarantees are financially sound. However, there is the possibility of an insurance company default, although this seems unlikely.

As is the case with other bonds, one of the key determinants of risk and yield is term to maturity. A portfolio of short-term municipal bonds usually carries less risk and yield than a portfolio of long-term municipal bonds.

Tax-Exempt Money Market Funds

Because these municipal bond funds invest in short-term municipal debt and usually offer checking privileges, they are effective, low-risk vehicles for tax-exempt investment and are competitive with savings accounts in terms of yield and liquidity. Low yields on these funds make them unattractive long-term investments, but they are useful places to "park" money during uncertain economic climates.

Tax-Exempt Bond Funds

A variety of funds have various mixes of portfolio maturities and types of securities chosen for investment. Some concentrate their attention on longer-term investments to secure higher yield or may be dedicated to zero-coupon securities maturing in a specific year. Some funds are devoted solely to investing in the state and local government debt of particular states in order to offer investors double or triple tax-free returns (as in the case of New York City residents). A table in the June 24, 1991, issue of *Forbes* shows the basis-point savings attributable to state tax rates if you invest in a double tax-free fund. This article also lists the names of recommended funds in each state. Vanguard Insured Funds are recommended in New York, New Jersey, and Pennsylvania, and Fidelity Tax Free Funds are recommended in Massachusetts, Michigan, and Minnesota. These no-load funds may be of interest to you if you reside in these states. Franklin Funds are recommended in seven states, but these funds carry a sales charge. See the article for other recommendations and more details about specific basis-point levels of savings.

How Would You Select a Municipal Fund Portfolio?

In this section we will choose an array of municipal bond funds from among funds which are exempt from federal taxes, without including funds devoted to specific states. If you wanted to do a comparison of funds which invest in a specific state's debt, you will find complete listings sorted by state in *Barron's* quarterly Lipper Gauge report on municipal bond funds. The sources of the array drawn for this analysis are *Forbes'* 9/3/90 listing of municipal bond funds and *Consumer Reports'* 6/90 listing of municipal bond funds.

Since short-term municipal bond funds on the *Consumer Reports* list have already been considered in Chapter 6, they will not be included here. Other no-load funds of average or better risk which have a portfolio quality rating no lower than A are shown in Table 9-1 (high-yield funds excluded) together with *Forbes'* "up" and "down" market ratings.

You will recall that maturities are an important factor in how bond funds behave. Since about one-half of the funds involve long-term bonds and do better in an up market, we can group these funds according to these characteristics when we proceed with our graphic analysis. This allows us to compare similar funds and avoids comparing long- and short-term funds.

As indicated by check marks on Figure 9-1, the best choices from among the longer-term maturity bond funds are SAFECO and Scudder. Vanguard Insured Long Term is not included because historical data were unavailable for the first 9 months of the period under consideration. Among the intermediate-term maturity funds, Vanguard Intermediate is clearly the first choice (see Table 9-2, page 183, and Figure 9-2, page 184).

Table 9-1. Municipal Bond Funds of Average or Better Risk

Average maturity (years)	*Consumer Reports'* quality A portfolio or better fund	*Forbes'* up market	*Forbes'* down market
21.0	SAFECO	A	C
8.8	Dreyfus Intermediate Tax Exempt	D	A
20.2	Vanguard Municipal—Long Term	A	D
18.0	Vanguard Municipal Insured—Long Term	A	C
19.8	Scudder Managed Municipal Bonds	B	D
22.8	Fidelity Municipal Bond	B	C
8.8	Vanguard Municipal Intermediate Term	D	B
24.0	Dreyfus Tax Exempt Bond	—	—
8.6	USAA Tax Exempt Intermediate Term	D	A
10.1	Fidelity Limited Term Municipal	D	B
24.4	T. Rowe Price Tax Free Income	C	D

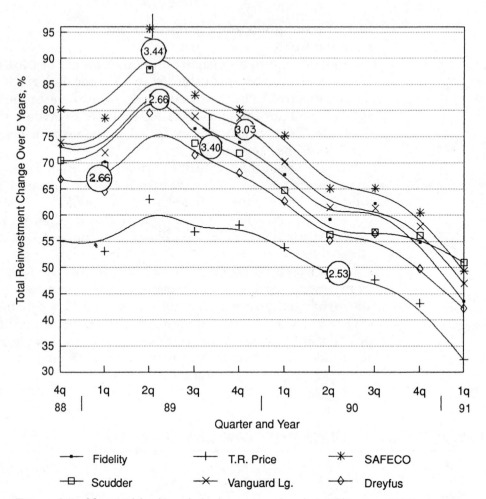

Figure 9-1. Municipal fund trends for longer-term bonds for 2½ years (total reinvestment percentage change over 5 years).

Summary of High-Tax-Avoidance Decision Steps

1. Decide on the tax avoidance strategy you want to pursue. Under certain circumstances, tax deferral may be preferred to tax-exempt investments, because of relatively lower yields on the latter, a drawback in capital accumulation plans.

2. If tax deferral is important in your tax avoidance approach, choose methods that are available to you and appropriate to your goals and circumstances. You may want to select more

Table 9-2. Performance Summary Table

Fund	Average 2½-year performance level, %	Performance instability	Risk-adjusted performance index
Dreyfus Tax Exempt Intermediate	54.12	7.08	—
USAA Tax Exempt Intermediate	52.46	7.26	−9.22
T. Rowe Price Tax Free Income	51.11	8.27	−2.53
Fidelity Limited Term Municipal	54.73	8.43	0.45
Vanguard Municipal Intermediate Term	61.97	8.51	5.49
Dreyfus Tax Exempt	61.62	10.40	2.26
Scudder Managed Municipal Bond*	65.80	10.52	3.40
Fidelity Municipal Bond	66.90	11.89	2.66
Vanguard Municipal— Long Term	69.14	12.03	3.03
SAFECO Municipal Bond**	73.23	12.64	3.44

*Best buy intermediate-term tax-exempt fund
**Best buy long-term tax-exempt funds

than one vehicle from among variable annuity and variable life contracts, IRAs, Keogh, and 401(k) plans.

3. If you decide to invest in tax-exempt municipal bond funds, consider the various sources of risk and the kind of underlying securities you want to invest in. Portfolio quality and maturity are key factors to consider.

4. From funds recommended by several sources, select an array of choices that meet the investment criteria you care about in choosing a tax-exempt fund.

5. Create a performance summary table and/or charts which portray graphically the recent investment performance of the array of funds you have selected. Make choices of the best-buy funds based on trends shown in the charts and/or on the risk-adjusted Performance Index.

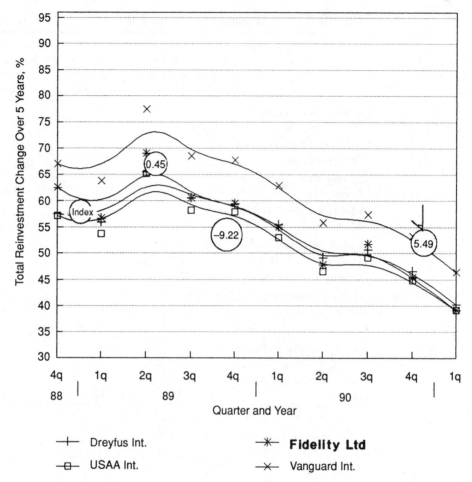

Figure 9-2. Municipal fund trends for intermediate-term funds for 2½ years (total reinvestment percentage change over 5 years).

10

An Illustration

At the end of Chapter 3 we presented a case study of the story of M which demonstrated how to use the financial planning approach that was developed in Chapters 2 and 3. At the conclusion of this example it was clear that M had specific goals and an investment strategy to achieve them. In this chapter you will see how M might use the portfolio selection approach recommended in Chapters 6 through 9 to carry out his investment strategy.

M Revisited

To recapitulate, M's current situation and future plans suggest that he invest $25,000, which he has available in cash, for 15 years, and continue to add savings of $10,000 annually to his investment portfolio until he retires 13 years from now. After considering his preferences, needs, and investment goals, M has devised the investment plan shown in Table 10-1.

M's First Transition Portfolio

In seeking to implement an investment plan for the first transition period, M also desires to pay attention to his needs for additional life insurance and tax advice, as identified by the quadrant analysis of investment prerequisites. Therefore, M chooses to pursue tax-deferred methods of capital accumulation through the use of an IRA and variable life contract and to take advantage of his employer's 401(k) supplementary pension plan. Because

Table 10-1. Summary of M's Investment Plan

Period	Importance rank of investment features	First choice of levels for each investment factor
First transition: present to 6 years from now (second daughter's wedding)	1. Growth	Moderate
	2. Risk	Moderate
	3. Tax avoidance	Moderate
	4. Income	Low
Second transition: 6 years from now to 13 years from now (retirement)	1. Growth	Moderate
	2. Risk	Low
	3. Tax avoidance	Moderate
	4. Income	Low
Third transition: 13 years from now to 25 years from now (death)	1. Risk	Low
	2. Income	Moderate
	3. Growth	Low
	4. Tax avoidance	None

growth is his first priority during this period, M would choose an array of funds similar to the array of high-growth funds discussed in Chapter 7. Assuming that M's analysis were identical to our own, the most desirable choices among this array would be IAI Regional and T. Rowe Price International Stock. In addition, the analysis presented in Chapter 6 suggested two funds that can be considered for low-risk and moderate-growth: the Dodge and Cox Balanced Fund and the Mathers Fund. In Chapter 7 we also recommended the inclusion of a well-managed S&P index fund, such as the Vanguard Index 500, in a high-growth portfolio.

In light of the economic conditions prevailing at the time of this writing, M would be well-advised to consider the following allocations of his present and future assets among the foregoing choices of mutual funds. We are assuming that this portfolio is being constructed at the end of 1990.

M is starting with $25,000 to be invested. Because M expects the economy to be gaining strength over the foreseeable future, he wants to invest most of his investable assets (rather than holding large parts in cash or gold or other defensive investments). He has identified four funds as mentioned above (two funds that he picked for growth potential and two that he picked for low risk and moderate growth. M reasons that he should hold a relatively small amount of cash (5 percent). Of course, in addition to his $25,000 of investable assets, he also has 6 months of income in emergency cash—bank accounts, certificates of deposit, and money market funds—that he could use in case of an emergency (medical bills, repairing the furnace, etc.). Since M's first priority is growth, he uses 50 percent of his $25,000 to buy his selected growth funds. At this point he decides to put 25 percent in IAI Regional and 25 percent in T. Rowe Price International Stock. He has now allocated 55 percent of his money. M will put the remaining money in the two funds he selected from Chapter 6 and in an S&P index fund. For want of a better distribution, he selects 15 percent to each of the three funds. So $25,000 of M's portfolio following our analysis would be as follows:

Cash (money market fund)	5%
IAI Regional	25
T. Rowe Price International Stock	25
Dodge and Cox Balanced Fund	15
Mathers Fund	15
Vanguard Index 500	15

The point to remember is that M might have allocated a larger percentage to cash if he expected the economy to be weak in the coming months. This would have protected against drops in the value of stocks and would have given him money to invest as the market improved. Although he is trying to invest for the long term and not trying to outguess the market, M is aware of external conditions and adjusts his investment strategy accordingly. For example, if M were convinced that stocks were now highly overvalued, he would put a substantial part of his investment in cash and wait for signs of improvement before shifting to stocks.

M's Second Transition Portfolio

M's second transition begins 6 years from now with the marriage of his second daughter, and we cannot foretell what the economic climate will be at that time. However, since the only change in investment strategy which M anticipates is a shift toward lower risk, we can imagine how he might respond to alternative economic scenarios. For example, if P-E ratios and long-term interest rates indicate he should move assets into bonds and out of stocks, M would choose to examine the low-risk and moderate-income choices recommended in Chapter 6 as additional alternatives to consider, even though he is still interested in growth as his first priority. The best among these might be Vanguard Fixed-Income Short-Term Bond. However, if long-term currency changes appeared to favor the yen over the dollar, M would be receptive to choosing an additional international fund, such as the Japan Fund, from among those recommended in Chapter 7. Risk may be reduced by changing allocations to funds suggested in the portfolio in Table 10-2.

For the second transition, we assume that M has succeeded in earning the 10 percent per year that he had estimated he could earn (see M's calculations). M now has $91,443 to invest for his second transition (after 6 years). We assume that his original choices turned out to be good ones, and he did not have to revise his choices during the past 6 years. Of course if the economic situation had changed drastically or if his personal situation had changed greatly, he would have reanalyzed his situation and made new choices. For example, if the economy took a turn for the worse, he would have considered a more defensive investment

Table 10-2. M's Second Transition Portfolio

Fund	$25,000 to invest, first transition, %	$91,443 to invest, second transition, %
Cash (money market fund)	5	10
IAI Regional	25	15
T. Rowe Price International Stock	25	15
Dodge & Cox Balanced	15	15
Mathers Fund	15	15
Vanguard Index 500	15	10
Vanguard Fixed-Income Short-Term Bond	0	10
Japan Fund	0	10

posture. If the economy had started to expand rapidly and the stock market had begun to look extremely promising, he would have considered moving to a more aggressively growth-oriented strategy.

M's Third Transition Portfolio

Changes in M's investment strategy during this period reflect the readjustments he faces during retirement. He needs to lower risk and move from growth toward income-producing investments. Choices recommended in Chapter 8 are now ripe for consideration. These include: Vanguard Fixed Income GNMA, Wellesley Income, and USAA Mutual Income. These selections could replace some of the more growth-oriented funds retained in M's portfolio during the preceding period. M also would want to delete international funds in the interest of risk reduction, although some growth is necessary to protect his assets against inflation and to accumulate legacies for his beneficiaries. Accordingly, portfolio allocation during retirement should be as shown in Table 10-3.

Table 10-3. M's Third Transition Portfolio

Fund	$91,443 to invest, second transition, %	$223,074 to invest, third transition, %
Cash (money market)	10	20
IAI Regional	15	0
T. Rowe Price International Stock	15	0
Dodge & Cox Balanced	15	0
Mathers Fund	15	0
Vanguard Index 500	10	10
Vanguard Fixed-Income Short-Term Bond	10	10
Japan Fund	10	0
Vanguard Fixed-Income GNMA	0	20
Wellesley Income	0	20
USAA Mutual Income	0	20

For M's retirement portfolio, once again we assume that the situation is as described in the fund selection chapters—not presuming to forecast how the thousands of mutual funds will have done by 13 years hence. So assume that M does the analysis as we described in previous chapters and decides that he will reallocate the money (now up to $223,074) to reflect his changing life situation as he enters retirement. He adds Vanguard Fixed Income GNMA, Wellesley Income, and USAA Mutual Income to reflect the need for retirement income. He also increases his cash allocation to reflect the more conservative investment stance that he is adopting as he enters his retirement years.

As we have seen in this illustration, mutual funds, combined with tax-deferral plans, are a practical means for implementing long-term investment plans which span several phases in a person's life. They may be used to manage investments wisely, even if you yourself are not a professional investment analyst or manager, by applying discretion, common sense, and research to make choices appropriate to your preferences, needs, and circumstances.

Epilogue: M's Reality Test

Would M have achieved his investment objectives if he had invested in the three portfolios described in this chapter? At this writing (February 1992), we can only judge performance during 1 year subsequent to 1990, the last year considered as a basis for M's decisions about portfolio selection. In reality, these choices were made by the authors prospectively, without regard to fund performance during 1991. If M had made his investments on January 1, 1991, his 1-year return on invested assets (excluding cash) on December 31, 1991, would have been:

First transition portfolio: 23%

Second transition portfolio: 18%

Third transition portfolio: 19%

On the cash portion, the average return on money market funds was under 6 percent, which was more than short-term bank certificates of deposit were yielding during this period.

How well did M's investments do in comparison to investments in other mutual funds? During 1991, a time of rising stock prices, the average return for all mutual funds was 23 percent, about the same as the return M achieved on his first transition portfolio, the most growth oriented of the three examples. Only 5 percent of total assets were held in cash in this portfolio, as is appropriate for someone with moderate growth and risk objectives during a rising market. M achieved his objectives by doing as well as the average mutual fund manager, without paying high sales charges because he invested in no-load funds.

During 1991, a time of declining interest rates, the average return for fixed income mutual funds was 18 percent, about the same as the return M achieved on his second- and third-transition portfolios. These portfolios were designed to provide lower risk than the first portfolio and may therefore be compared to this lower-risk performance standard. Once again, M equalled the performance of the average mutual fund fund manager in a category to which his selections may be compared, without paying high sales charges.

Although M's portfolio choices yielded about average performance compared to other mutual fund performance, they far exceeded returns on the "cash" portion of his assets.

It is important to keep in mind that M has retained his independence by limiting himself to no-load investments. M is not "locked-in" by fear of incurring a loss associated with high sales charges he has already paid or by substantial exit fee penalties, called "back-end loads." As a result, M may continue to actively manage his personal financial plans and mutual fund portfolios as external conditions change and his own needs and circumstances evolve.

PART 4

Additional Resources and Other Topics

In Chapter 11, you will find a discussion of additional resources and topics that will be of interest as you begin to take responsibility for making your own investment decisions. These include a comprehensive discussion of fund families and managers, and printed, computer, and other resources, including a brief bibliography.

11
Continue to Improve Your Investment Results

You have now been through a process of identifying and clarifying your financial goals and you have learned how to produce a definite plan to achieve your goals. You have also learned how to select a portfolio of mutual funds that will enable you to achieve your goals. Information is the key resource to continuing and improving your investment results. Much of this chapter will provide additional investment information or tell you where to go for such information.

In addition, this chapter will help you to decide how to proceed from here, supplying some information about books, magazines, and other sources of information that will supplement what you have learned here. Chapter 11 will also give you some helpful advice about evaluating your results and about such matters as how to read prospectuses and how you can use your computer to help with your investing and financial planning.

Fund Families

Most funds belong to fund families, groups of funds that are operated and managed by the same management organization (although each individual fund may have its own investment objective and its own group of specific individuals who pick the securities and monitor their performance). In looking at which funds to invest in, consider not only the specific fund in which you are interested but also the family to which the fund belongs. A number of fund groups offer a wide range of funds of different types. This could be an advantage if you decide to switch to a different type of fund. Switching from one fund to another within the same family of funds is usually relatively easy and inexpensive, though some fund families discourage frequent switching by imposing extra charges. In most cases the switch to another fund in the family can be done immediately with a telephone call to the fund management company. It is more difficult to switch to another family. If your chosen fund belongs to a large family, it may be advisable to look at the performance of some of the other funds in the family before sending your money. If another family has a roughly equivalent fund (to the one you are interested in investing in), the performance of other funds in the family may influence where you should invest—unless you are certain that you have no interest in switching.

You might also want to investigate programs that some discount brokerage firms offer. These allow you to buy no-load and low-load funds through the brokerage firm and switch money easily among the funds in the broker's program. The convenience of switching easily among fund families (for funds that happen to be in the program) comes at the price of an additional fee, which will, of course, reduce your return. You need to decide whether the convenience is worth the extra charge. One such program, by the Charles Schwab company, offers more than 400 funds.

There are many fund families, including some very large ones with tens of billions of dollars invested in its funds. Many of these families offer both load funds and no-load funds.

Overall, the 10 largest mutual fund families (in alphabetical order) are:

Capital Group
Dean Witter
Dreyfus
Federated
Fidelity

Franklin

Kemper

Merrill Lynch

Shearson Lehman/IDS

Vanguard

You are probably already familiar with at least some of these names. Many of the funds offered by these families are load funds. At the end of 1991 there were 50 families of no-load funds that had $350 million or more of investors' funds. Some of these no-load groups also offered some load funds. The top 17 no-load families (those with no-load funds assets of more than $3 billion) are listed in Table 11-1.

Table 11-1. Top No-Load Families

Fund	$ millions
Benham Management	8,590
Dreyfus	44,598
Federated Research	11,518
Fidelity Management & Research	103,677
Financial (Invesco Funds)	4,910
Janus Capital Corp.	6,014
Mutual Series Funds	4,150
Neuberger & Berman	4,475
Nicholas Co. Inc.	3,062
T. Rowe Price Associates	22,307
Schwab Funds	8,462
Scudder, Stevens & Clark	19,241
Stein Roe & Farman	4,108
Strong/Corneliuson	3,183
Twentieth Century	14,994
USAA Investment Management	9,049
Vanguard Group	77,842

NOTE: Data provided as of December 31, 1991.

SOURCE: Table provided by Sheldon Jacobs, publisher of *Handbook for No-Load Fund Investors*.

Sketches of Several Major Fund Families

Fidelity.   Fidelity is the giant of mutual fund families with well over 100 funds of all types and specialties. Its Magellan Fund is probably the best-known and most successful of all mutual funds. In mid-1991, Fidelity's Magellan Fund was surpassed, as the fund with the best record over a 10-year period, by another Fidelity fund which invests in health-care stocks.

T. Rowe Price.   T. Rowe Price of Baltimore is a long-established manager of a group of no-load funds. In addition to the normal types of funds, T. Rowe Price offers an option called the Spectrum Funds. Investors who are just starting to invest in mutual funds or are unsure about how to select a portfolio can choose Spectrum Growth Fund or Spectrum Income Fund (or both). T. Rowe Price money managers will then make the decisions about how to allo-cate the money among the various T. Rowe Price mutual funds in the way that they think is appropriate at the current time. They also reevaluate and move the money as they think appropriate. The Spectrum Growth fund invests in T. Rowe Price stock funds, and the Spectrum Income Fund invests in T. Rowe Price income funds.

Dreyfus.   Dreyfus is one of the best-known fund families to the general public as a result of its ubiquitous commercials featuring its mascot lion emerging from the subway. Dreyfus is known for clever marketing and for in 1974 erecting the first direct-mar-keted no-load money market fund, the Dreyfus Liquid Assets fund. The fund enabled small investors to get money market rates for the first time. When rates soared in the high inflation years of the 1970s, the money poured in. Dreyfus sells primarily fixed in-come funds but, after buying a small bank in New Jersey in 1983, also began offering banking products in several states, although it sold its credit card business in 1989. Dreyfus also offers an asset allocation proposal for investors who complete an application questionnaire with questions about their investment experience, stage of life, investment goals, total assets, risk tolerance, tax situ-ation, and investment history.

Twentieth Century.   Twentieth Century Investors is best known for two of its funds that have ranked high in many fund performance lists. Its Select fund and its Growth fund (which have slightly different investment objectives but both aim for long-term growth) have both shown up on many high-performance lists. Twentieth Century has long had a policy of encouraging small investors by requiring no minimum investment amount but has placed some restrictions on very small accounts in recent years.

USAA.   USAA funds are sponsored by the USAA insurance operation, which was established to sell insurance by mail to military and former military officers. Operating through the mail, USAA maintains an efficient, low-cost operation for selling financial services to its specialized group of customers.

Vanguard.   Based in Valley Forge, Pennsylvania, this fund family has gained a reputation for having a very efficient operation which permits it to have among the lowest fees of any fund family. The low fees also contribute to the good performance of its funds. Vanguard's funds are all no-load. A *Fortune* article comparing how the 10 largest mutual fund families performed in investment results called Vanguard the "clear winner."[1]

Fund Managers and Other Notable Investors

Peter Lynch.   An article on Peter Lynch, who was ending a 13-year period as head of the world's biggest mutual fund, stated that few people in any career have enjoyed the degree of success that he has had.[2] Lynch's $20 billion Magellan Fund had been the most successful of all mutual funds over the period during which he managed it. Its total return to its investors over those 13 years was 2510 percent, or over 28 percent compound annual return (as compared to 451 percent for the Dow Jones average). Lynch started with Fidelity in the summer of 1966. He was one of 100 applicants for the job and attributes his success in being hired to the fact that he had caddied for the president of the company. During his tenure as head of Magellan, Lynch put in 85-hour

[1]Andrew Evan Serwer, "Who Is the Best Manager for Your Money?" *Personal Investing,* June 17, 1991, pp. 25, 26.

[2]Peter Lynch, "Money and Markets," *Fortune,* April 23, 1991, pp. 197–200.

weeks and travelled and read annual reports constantly in search of good investment possibilities. Lynch has said that he often felt good as a result of knowing that many small investors had made a lot of money in his fund, and he continually worried about the responsibility he felt to keep up the good record. A $10,000 investment in Magellan Fund on the day Lynch took charge would have grown to $270,000 by 1990. Incidentally, the Magellan Fund is not a no-load—it charges a 3 percent load. Despite the $20 million or so of personal wealth which Lynch accumulated, he lives simply and now spends his time running a $7 million charitable foundation he established.

Warren Buffett.   If you had given Warren Buffett $10,000 to invest for you in 1956, you would now have about $35 million. Warren Buffett, sometimes called the "oracle of Omaha," is the CEO of Berkshire Hathaway, Inc. Buffett bought Berkshire Hathaway, a relatively small textile company, and turned it into an investment company (in which he owns the controlling interest) by selling off the textile business and various other operations and buying a portfolio of businesses which he judged to be especially appealing. The basic businesses of Berkshire Hathaway are very profitable and produce a steady flow of cash which Buffett invests so expertly. Buffett is no in-and-out investor. Buffett buys excellent companies that he expects to hold for a long time. He is a disciple of Benjamin Graham with whom he studied at Columbia University. His personal holdings are worth about $4 billion, yet he lives simply in the same house he has owned since the 1950s and rejects the idea that he should lavish wealth on his children—either now or at his death. Berkshire Hathaway stock is sold on the New York Stock Exchange, where it is one of the highest-priced stocks (about $8500 a share in July 1991). The company's annual meeting in Omaha, each spring, has become a celebrated event where Buffett philosophizes and greets his investors—many of whom he has made rich. In 1991, following a scandal in treasury securities trading involving Salomon Brothers, Warren Buffett took over as CEO to protect his major investment in the firm. In 1992, after seeing Salomon through the worst part of this debacle, he installed a new CEO but continues to have a role in managing the company.

John Templeton.   John Templeton was born in a poor family in Tennessee. He struggled to finish Yale during the Depression, then won a Rhodes scholarship to Oxford. During 1939 he decided that stocks would soon rebound and borrowed money to transact a remarkable stock trade—he ordered $100 worth of every stock selling for under $1, including stocks of bankrupt companies. The trade cost him about $10,000 but he was able to sell the stocks for $40,000 within a few years, winning on his hunch that the economy would improve and the stock markets would rebound from their Depression levels as the world moved toward war. After several more years of building a reputation as an investor, he moved to Nassau in the Bahamas and began compiling a great record with his Templeton Growth Fund. Pioneering in investing internationally, during the 1960s and 1970s his fund had the best record of all mutual funds. Furthermore, it did well in both up and down markets and showed that profits could be reaped from overseas investments as well as investments in America. In recent years he has been interested in religion and has established a foundation which awards a prize (currently worth about $800,000) for "progress in religion."

John Neff. John Neff is not well known outside of the investment community. He lives in Berwyn, Pennsylvania, a main line suburb of Philadelphia, and runs the Windsor fund. Neff is highly regarded by other investment professionals who have voted him their choice in surveys as the one they would like to have manage their own money. Over a period of 24 years he produced a 14.3 percent compound rate of return at Windsor compared to 9.4 percent for the Standard and Poor's 500 index. So Neff would have yielded about $247,000 on a $10,000 investment, whereas the stock market would have returned about $86,000. Neff grew up during the Depression and lived in Michigan and Texas (he was born in Ohio). While studying marketing at the University of Toledo he discovered that he had a gift for investing money. This occurred while he was studying with a teacher who updated Graham and Dodd's famous book on security analysis. After working as a security analyst for a Cleveland bank, Neff moved to Wellington Management in Philadelphia in 1963. A year later he became the head of the 6-year-old fund now called the Vanguard Windsor Fund. In addition to his stellar record as a mutual fund manager, Neff took charge of the University of Pennsylvania endowment fund in 1980. Before Neff took over, the fund had compiled one of the worst records of all college endowments. Neff quickly made it one of the top performers.

Benjamin Graham. Benjamin Graham is most remembered for two books, *The Intelligent Investor* (a classic about how to invest in stocks) and *Security Analysis* (the standard text, written with Donald Dodd, on how to analyze the value of stocks). Graham came to the United States from England at age 1 in 1895. His father died when he was 9. He was a good student and mastered the classics and mathematics. He loved great literature and often quoted from it. He had broad interests, ranging far beyond Wall Street, that included philosophy, languages, tennis, skiing, dancing, and philosophy of religions (although he himself professed no religious faith). His analytical techniques relied on mathematical analysis of the business (ratios, percentages, growth rates, etc.) rather than a knowledge of the management or other more qualitative or intuitive considerations. Security analysis became a systematic, mathematical science in Graham's hands. From 1928 to 1956 Graham taught at Columbia Business School, where Warren Buffett, among others, met him and was influenced by his investment training. Buffett extended the Graham techniques by, among other things, adding his concepts of the value of a well-known franchise (such as Coca Cola, Kirby Vacuum Cleaners, and the *Washington Post*).

T. Rowe Price. The name of T. Rowe Price, who died in 1983, lives on in the firm T. Rowe Price Associates, Inc., of Baltimore (a venerable manager of a family of no-load funds which he started in 1950) and in the investment approach that he created. Price was highly disciplined (to the point of inflexibility) and driven by the need to be a superior investor and to be seen by others as superior. His associates remember him as extremely able but irascible and egotistical and unwilling to be involved in any activity unless he could be in charge.

How to Read a Prospectus

The prospectus gives you information that will help you to decide if a fund is right for you. The fund managers are required to provide you with a copy of the prospectus for your protection before you invest in the fund. It will give you some basic information that you need about the investment objectives of the fund and about the loads and the fees it charges you for managing your money. This will allow you to determine if the fund is right for you. Unfortunately, although fund managers have made some progress in improving the writing in prospectuses, most are still written in a forbidding "legalese" that many people find boring or intimidating. To get to the truly valuable information, you generally have to wade through a great deal of uninformative verbiage. Your goal in reading the prospectus is to locate the crucial information that will confirm or contradict your prior perceptions about the fund.

The first two or three pages give some of the key information:

- Cost data presented in a standardized form, including the sales charge (or load) if there is one and the charges that management exacts for running the fund
- The record of the fund
- Management fees (which management charges you for managing the fund)
- Expenses (these should be low)

Also check the objectives of the fund and any restrictions on trading (also called "switching"). This is important if you expect to move to other funds in the family, but in most fund families the limitations are not a problem unless you make frequent switches.

And of course, you should confirm your understanding of the objectives of the fund—presumably you have some ideas of what they are before you get to this stage. Other things you might want to check in the prospectus include instructions on setting up IRAs or other retirement accounts or buying and selling shares.

If you like reading prospectuses and yearn for more, you can request another document from the fund manager that gives more financial detail, known as the "Statement of Additional Information." You should also check this information against some of the other references sources listed in this book, or call the fund if you need more information.

How Do You Evaluate Your Results?

On the surface evaluating results might seem to be no problem at all. After all, most mutual funds tout their numbers in graphs that show how much you would have made if you had invested in their fund 10 years ago or 20 years ago. Also, any mutual fund today has computers that are quite capable of calculating your effective yield over the time you have held the fund, taking into consideration your additions and withdrawals. Furthermore, many investors have their own computers (and software) at home or in their offices that can make the required calculations. The difficulty is that the charts, showing results that the fund families advertise, are only valid for investors who invested a lump sum on the initial day of the illustration, and reinvested all dividends until the last date shown. Obviously few, if any, mutual fund owners would have exactly this purchase history for their own purchases. Most mutual fund holders, especially over long periods such as the 10, 20, or 30 years often used in these illustrations, have added or withdrawn money or even gotten out and then come back to the fund—perhaps switching to another fund in the same family before returning.

In such situations, with complex histories for each customer, it is not easy to provide a single number that gives the yield of the account. This is what customers presumably want so that they can compare their results with the yields on bank CDs or money market funds or Treasuries and determine if their fund is giving an adequate return. Although it is not easy to do such calculations, the fund family's computers could easily be programmed to do the calculation for each fund of each individual and even for the portfolio of funds that each fund holder has with that fund family. Since few funds provide this information, fund managers apparently feel that fund holders do not want the information or that it would cost too much to provide or would raise too many questions about the funds' performance. In any event, if you want the information, you will have to calculate it yourself. The exact calculation must consider the timing of each transaction that involves adding cash to the account or taking cash out of the account. Although the calculation involves only some fairly advanced arithmetic, it can involve a lot of calculation and extensive recordkeeping if the account is large or active or for extensive portfolios of funds. To complicate matters, even if you could manage to find a fund family that will provide the yield calculations for their fund holders, it would not help much if you also have funds in other fund families. If you are a sophisticated spreadsheet user or are familiar with financial calculations, you can undoubtedly develop a spreadsheet, or a worksheet for use with a financial calculator, for computing the internal rate of return for your portfolio.

For most fund holders, the best answer to this problem is to use an approximate method that considerably simplifies the calculation and gives a fairly accurate estimate of the percentage return. Such methods are described in the October 1989 issue of *Money* magazine and in the *Handbook for No-load Fund Investors*.[3] You might also want to write to your fund manager and ask that they provide this calculation for their investors.

Printed Resources

Important sources of up-to-date information to help guide you with your mutual fund investing are periodical publications. Many magazines, newspapers, and other periodicals deal with mutual funds, investments, and related matters, including:

Barron's

Business Week

Kiplinger's Personal Finance Magazine (formerly *Changing Times*)

Forbes

Fortune

Investor's Daily

Money

U.S. News and World Report

Wall Street Journal

Consumer Reports

Financial World

Broadcast Resources

There are also many broadcast sources. Just a few of the many such broadcast sources include:

"Louis Rukeyser's Wall Street Week" (on PBS)

"Adam Smith's Money World" (on PBS)

[3]Sheldon Jacobs, *Handbook for No-Load Fund Investors,* No-Load Fund Investors, Inc., Hastings-on-Hudson, New York, 1991, pp. 130–131.

"The Nightly Business Report" (PBS)

"Market Place" (The American Public Radio's daily business program)

CNBC (the cable channel that is largely devoted to financial and consumer-related programs)

Further Reading

These are the books we like most on mutual funds investing:

Chambers, Larry, and Kenn Miller: *The First Time Investor: Starting out Safe and Smart*, Probus Publishing, Chicago, 1991.

Dorf, Richard C.: *The New Mutual Fund Investment Advisor*, Probus Publishing, Chicago, 1988.

Headington-McGee, Judith, and Jerrold Dickson: *J. K. Lasser's Personal Investment Annual 1990-1991: Build Long-Term Wealth and Financial Security*, J. K. Lasser Institute, a division of Simon & Schuster, Inc., New York, Glenview, Illinois, 1989.

Lerner, Joel: *Financial Planning for the Utterly Confused*, rev. ed., McGraw-Hill, New York, 1988.

Norling, Darrell, Karen Hess, and Karen Nystrom: *Your Financial Planning Kit*, Wiley, New York, 1989.

Pond, Jonathan: *Jonathan Pond's Guide to Investment and Financial Planning: A Timely Reference for Improving Your Financial Life*, NYIF Corp./ Simon & Schuster, New York, 1991.

Pritchard, Robert E., Gregory C. Potter, and Larry E. Howe: *Be Your Own Financial Advisor*, Prentice-Hall, Englewood Cliffs, New Jersey, 1988.

Raphaelson, Elliot, and Debra Raphaelson West: *How to Be Your Own Financial Planner—Preparing for Retirement*, Scott Foresman, 1990.

Renberg, Werner, and Jeremiah Blitzer: *Making Money with Mutual Funds*, Wiley, New York, 1988.

Rosenberg, R. Robert, and Ralph V. Naples: *Outline of Personal Finance* (Schaum's Outline Series), McGraw-Hill, New York, 1976.

Ross, Joel: *Mutual Funds: Taking the Worry Out of Investing*, Prentice-Hall, Englewood Cliffs, New Jersey, 1988.

Rugg, Donald D.: *New Strategies for Mutual Fund Investing*, Dow Jones-Irwin, Homewood, Illinois, 1989.

Investment Classics

Some books about money and investing have become virtual classics. Although these books will not necessarily help you to pick specific investments or help you with the mechanics of investing, they present invaluable background for someone who wants to understand how markets work or what kinds of factors will influence the value of their investments or how greatly successful money managers have approached their work.

Although at least a dozen books could qualify as an investment classic, we have selected the following seven as our choices. Time spent reading any of these books will be well spent and will enrich your understanding of how to be a more thoughtful and ultimately (quite probably) a more successful investor.

Graham, Benjamin: *The Intelligent Investor,* Harper & Row, New York, 1986.

Little, Jeffrey B., and Lucien Rhodes: *Understanding Wall Street,* Liberty House, 1978.

Lynch, Peter, with John Rothchild: *One Up On Wall Street: How to Use What You Already Know to Make Money in the Market,* Simon & Schuster, New York, 1989.

Mackay, Charles: *Extraordinary Popular Delusions and the Madness of Crowds,* Farrar, Straus and Giroux; modern reprint of the 1841 classic.

Malkiel, Burton G.: *A Random Walk down Wall Street,* W. W. Norton & Co., 1990.

Smith, Adam: *The Money Game,* Random House, New York, 1967.

Train, John: *The Money Masters: Nine Great Investors: Their Winning Strategies and How You Can Apply Them,* Perennial Library/Harper & Row, New York, 1980.

More Advanced Reading

For readers who have a strong background in mathematics, a classic work that is not easy reading but will reward the effort is

Markowitz, Harry M.: *Portfolio Selection: Efficient Diversification of Investments,* Basil Blackwell, Cambridge, Massachussetts, 1991.

Newsletters

A number of newsletters are devoted to mutual fund investing. Although some of these are quite expensive, the serious mutual fund investor may find one of these worthwhile:

The No-load Fund Investor (monthly), Dobbs Ferry, N.Y. Includes lists of top no-load funds, tips, news, and performance comparisons. Also suggests portfolios of funds for various types of investors such as the wealth builder, the investor in the preretirement phase, or the retired investor.

Mutual Fund Values, a Chicago-based newsletter published by Morning Star.

Sources of Additional Information

For in-depth mutual fund information, these books are invaluable:

American Association of Individual Investors: *The Individual Investor's Guide to No-Load Mutual Funds,* International Publishing Corporation, Chicago, published annually.

Morningstar's Mutual Fund Values, Morningstar, Inc., Chicago, published biweekly.

The Handbook for No-Load Fund Investors, compiled by the editors of *The No-Load Fund Investor,* P.O. Box 283, Hastings-on Hudson, New York.

Jay Schabacker: *Jay Schabacker's Mutual Fund Buying Guide,* Phillips Publishing, Potomac, Maryland, published quarterly.

Standard and Poor's/Lipper Mutual Fund Profiles, McGraw-Hill, New York, published quarterly.

Computers and Investing

If you have access to a computer equipped with a modem, you may want to use it to track your investments. You will be able to get a vast amount of investment information through computer bulletin boards and on-line data services.

Many computer bulletin boards offer investment forums where you can exchange investment ideas and get answers to your investment questions. Some also allow you to download public domain investment software. On line data services include Prodigy, CompuServe, and GEnie. These have forums that deal with investing, give stock or mutual fund quotes, and give information about business developments.

Many computer programs are available for planning your investments, and new ones are being released all the time. Some examples include:

Checkwrite Plus

Managing Your Money

Quicken

Wealth Starter

Wealth Builder

Some of the above products will help with other aspects of your finances, such as budgeting. Check with your software dealer or with software write-ups in computer publications for more details and for the latest additions to this list.

There are also a number of programs that will help you prepare your tax returns:

Turbo Tax

Mac in Tax

Mac in Tax for Windows

Swiftax

Tax Cut

Other Data

Business Week magazine publishes computer disks of mutual fund data under the name the *Mutual Fund Scoreboard*. These disks include data on 900 equity and 750 fixed equity funds. Similar disks can also be obtained from several other sources as advertised on financial programs on cable TV or in financial publications.

Other Services

Among the discount stockbrokers that provide a mutual fund transaction service, the best-known is offered by Charles Schwab, the largest discounter. In mid-1991, the service was offering over 450 no-load and low-load funds and 24-hour order taking. You can move money easily between stock investments and mutual fund investments. Charles Schwab takes care of the recordkeeping, reinvesting or accumulation of dividends, moving dividends to money market funds so they will earn interest, and even buying funds on margin (which we do not recommend for the beginning investor). For current details and an explanation of charges and fees, call Charles Schwab or other discount brokers offering such plans.

Index

About the Authors

HOWARD KELLER is a financial analyst and business and strategic planner for Metropolitan Life in New York City. He is an NASD registered representative.

HARVEY SONTAG specializes in the area of consumer financial services for Metropolitan Life. He is the author of *Corporate Perceptions*.